# POCKET SIZE 4



## THE STORY TREE

*The Akiko Series,*
*Issues 19~25*



SIRIUS ENTERTAINMENT
UNADILLA, NEW YORK

*This book is dedicated*
*to my Kouji & Minae*
*Hirabayashi*

AKIKO POCKET SIZE 4 FEBRUARY, 2006.
FIRST PRINTING. PUBLISHED BY SIRIUS ENTERTAINMENT, INC.
LAWRENCE SALAMONE, PRESIDENT. ROBB HORAN, PUBLISHER.
KEITH DAVIDSEN, EDITOR. CORRESPONDENCE: P.O. BOX X, UNADILLA, NY 13849.

PRINTED IN THE USA.

My name is Akiko. Today I want to tell you about the day my friends from the planet Smoo came to visit me here on earth. I was happy to see them, but I knew we had to be careful not to be seen by too many people.

So we held a meeting in my bedroom and decided to go way out to the countryside where no one could bother us. Then for the rest of the day all we did was just sit around telling stories under this great, big tree...

I tell ya, 'Kiko, this is the life...
Now I know why ya keep comin' **back** to this planet!

You like it, huh?
Well, it could use a few more **monsters** here and there, just to keep it interesting...
That's probably why it still ain't in any of the guidebooks!
OF THE TWO HUNDRED EIGHTY SEVEN PLANETS I'VE BEEN TO, MA'AM, THIS IS ONE OF THE MOST HOSPITABLE.
Thanks, Gax.
Hey, Beeba. Why don't you tell us about the time you went to that place with the guy and you were lookin' for that thing?
You're speaking in complete sentences, Spuckler. That's **good.**
Now if we could only introduce you to the glamorous world of *proper* nouns...
C'mon, Beebs. You know what I'm talking about. The little guy with the two extra arms...
Oh, you must mean old **Gwum.**
Heavens! No one wants to hear ***that*** story again.
Sure we do. It sounds cool!
What was the name of that thing you were lookin' for?
The Hams n' Butter?

*The Hemmin Spotter*, Spuckler. It is perhaps the greatest work of literature in the history of the universe!
Go on. Tell us the story, Mr. Beeba.
Okay, okay!
But I'm warning you: it hasn't got a happy ending...

It all began many years ago, when I was still a student at the secluded University of Malbadoo. Most of the other students had gone home for the midyear recess, but I stayed behind in order to pursue my private passion: reading *The Hemmin Spotter*.

A fascinating tale of heroism and tragedy, *The Hemmin Spotter* was hampered only by the fact that its anonymous author chose not to include the last chapter, but instead buried it in an undisclosed location. Like hundreds before me, I idealistically threw myself into the task of discerning the final chapter's location by analysing the text for hidden clues...

"Taking Lirial in his arms, Gilgabud kissed her trembling lips, giving in at last to the torrent of emotions within him."
Trembling lips...
trembling lips...
There must be some kind of double meaning...
At it again, eh, Bobo?
I wish you'd stop calling me that, Gwum.
The use of that nickname was amusing back in middle school, but now that I'm pursuing a masters degree, I think that "sir" will do quite nicely, thank you.
How about "Sir Bobo?"
I said masters degree, Gwum, not knighthood.
Sainthood is more like it, Bobo...
...what with all the time you spend holed up here with that old book.

This "old book," my friend, is more valuable than ***you*** are.
It is one of only five remaining copies known to exist in this galaxy!
Really.
Mubla milk, Bobo?
That cheap swill you're drinking causes ***intestinal diseases*** in laboratory animals.
If you spent a little more time ***reading*** the books you haul around all day you'd ***know*** these things...
I only like books with pictures in them.
Or at least a few pages of scenes from the movie.
I'll bet the books you read aren't as spellbinding as ***this:***
"Brandishing the magic sword of Zandiron, Gilgabud stood before his hated enemy Rognor at last, certain that only one of them would walk away alive."
Who wins?
What do you mean, "who wins?!" That's not the ***point***, Gwum.
You're supposed to relish the ***dramatic tension.***
Tension, schmension.
I want the final score.

Yes, well you're not the only one, Gwum.
What I just read to you is the very last sentence of the book.
See? Not another word.
Jeez. What a time to get writer's block.
No, you fool. There **is** a final chapter. It's just not included in the book.
Sounds like a big marketing scam to me.
I'm telling you, Bobo, you've got to try this Mubla milk. It goes down **really** smooth.
Leave me alone, Gwum. I was just on the verge of a very insightful...
...er, insight.
Come on.
Just a sip!
SPLOP!
NO!!!
FUP FUP FUP

You stupid twit! You've got four hands, for heaven's sake! Can't you even hold onto a miserable little cup?!
This book was in mint condition! It's worth nothing now!
It's...
I could have gone on berating old Gwum for several more minutes, but it turned out that his ineptitude was a blessing in disguise..
...it's...
...it's a miracle!
I had no idea Mubla milk could make such unsightly stains.
Stains?!
Why, Gwum, old friend, this is a map!
It shows the precise location of The Hemmin Spotter's last chapter!

Is there a coupon or something you can mail in?
No, Gwum, don't you see? Now that we know where the manuscript is buried, all we have to do is go and dig it up!
What do you mean, "we?"
Gwum, I can't do this alone. I'll need all the help I can get.
Have you already forgotten how I helped you study for the Virpluck exam last semester?
I **failed** the Virpluck exam, Bobo!
Yes, but that's not **my** fault!
Come on, Gwum. You don't know what this manuscript is **worth**...
If we find it, we'll be rich as kings!
"Rich as kings?"
Was it *really* worth that much money?
Who said anything about money?
I was speaking ***figuratively.***
I don't know, Mr. Beeba. It sounds to me like you were trying to trick him.
"Trick" is a rather *harsh* term, Akiko.
I wanted to **motivate** the fellow...
...but you can't measure the rewards one gains from great literature in terms of vulgar, monetary figures.
See, that's what I like about this story.
No money. No jewels. Just a dusty old book.
I get a kick out of it 'cause the whole thing's jus' so goldurned ***stupid.***

*Ahem.* Gwum finally agreed to come with me, so we took the next boat to shore and began the arduous journey on foot.

Before long we were making our way along a stony ravine, still many miles from our final destination.

What's that over the next ridge, Bobo?

It looks like some sort of fortress...

You're right, Gwum!

Let's see if we can't get a closer look...

Scrambling over the ridge, we realized that this was a fortress unlike any we'd ever seen before...

Incredible! They must be a nomadic tribe of some sort!
Do you think they're friendly?
CHAK CHAK CHAK CHAK CHAK CHAK
Hold that thought, will you, Gwum?
Without so much as a word of greeting, a group of men came down and surrounded us.
With spears at our backs, we were brusquely escorted up the stairs...
...and through the main doors of the massive fortress.

We were then unceremoniously tossed into a detention cell and left to appraise the situation on our own.
"Rich as kings!"
Hunted down like **animals** is more like it!
I **knew** I shouldn't have agreed to this ridiculous quest of yours.
Gads! We're almost out of Mubla milk...
Have faith, Gwum. If I'm not mistaken, this moving fortress is going to take us straight to the manuscript itself!
Watch yourself, Bobo...
...there's a point at which cheerful optimism degenerates into garden-variety lunacy!
Here, Gwum.
I'll show you what I'm getting at.
See this symbol on the map? It stands for *Amnolia*, the final chapter of *The Hemmin Spotter.*
Well, if you were keeping your eyes open, you'd have noticed that this whole fortress is **festooned** with the symbol!
Point being?
**Think** about it, Gwum. Why would a band of nomads decorate their fortress with the *Amnolia* symbol?
Clearly, they're nothing more than a bunch of *Hemmin Spotter* enthusiasts like us!
***"Us?!"***
Your cavalier use of pronouns is really beginning to **bother** me, Bobo.

I imagine they're on their way to uncover the manuscript right now.
All we have to do is tag along and get hold of it before they do!
Now you listen to **me,** Bobo: these men are heavily armed!
**You** may be willing to risk your neck stealing a silly little book out from under their noses, but I want no part of it!
Backing out on me, are you?
Well...
...I'll have to do it ***alone,*** then.
In the late afternoon we were brought before the leader of the tribe, a mighty chieftain by the name of Mordloff.
Foul creatures...
...soil not my ears with the filth of your wretched names.
If in my presence to open your mouths you dare...
...it should be to offer but a single reason why your insignificant lives should be spared this day.
Speak well and may your words be nimble, for a man of little patience am I, and of mercy, lesser still.

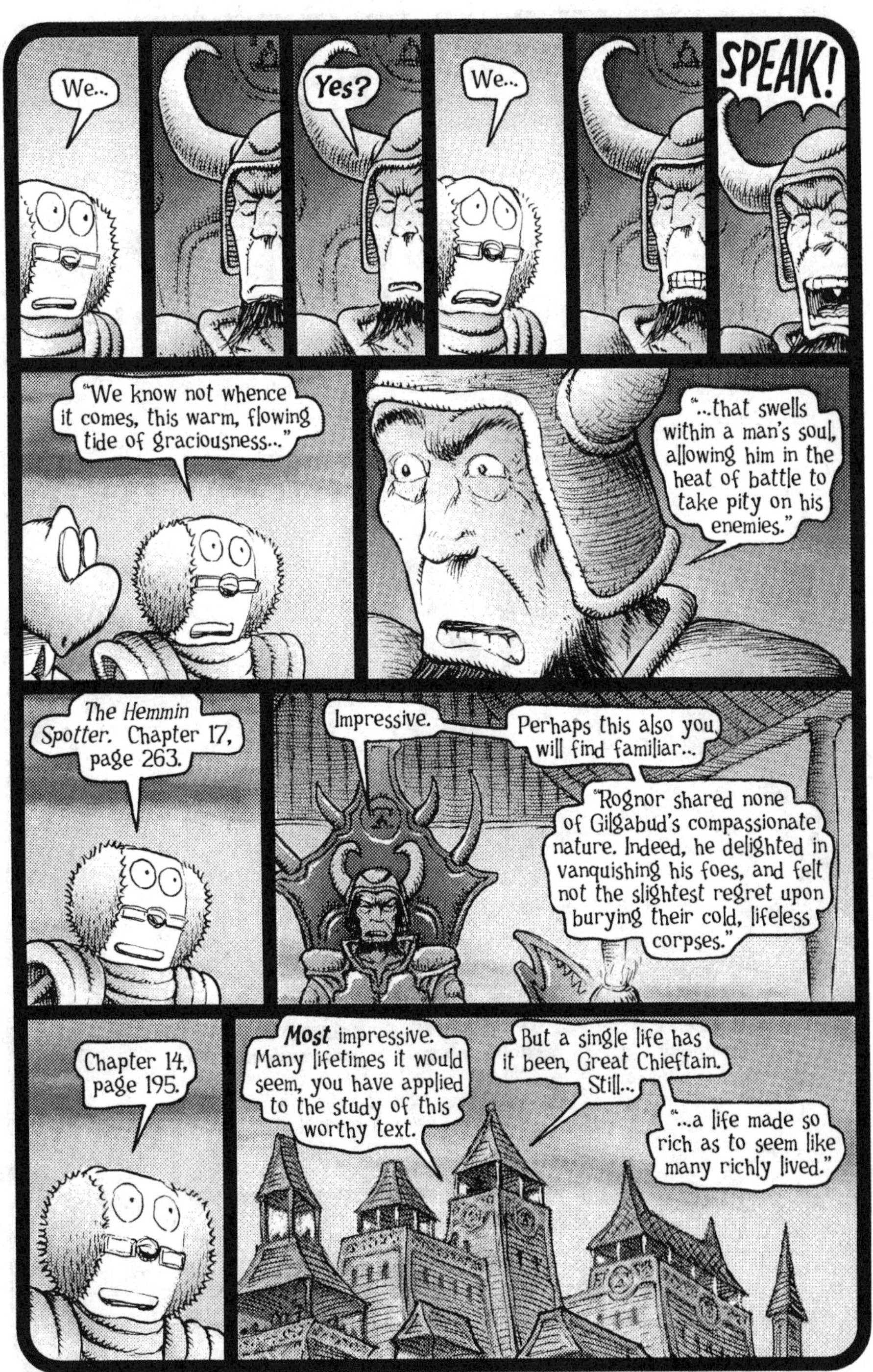

We...
Yes?
We...
SPEAK!
"We know not whence it comes, this warm, flowing tide of graciousness..."
"...that swells within a man's soul, allowing him in the heat of battle to take pity on his enemies."
The Hemmin Spotter. Chapter 17, page 263.
Impressive.
Perhaps this also you will find familiar...
"Rognor shared none of Gilgabud's compassionate nature. Indeed, he delighted in vanquishing his foes, and felt not the slightest regret upon burying their cold, lifeless corpses."
Chapter 14, page 195.
Most impressive. Many lifetimes it would seem, you have applied to the study of this worthy text.
But a single life has it been, Great Chieftain. Still...
"...a life made so rich as to seem like many richly lived."

Never before have I encountered a man from whose tongue the words of *The Hemmin Spotter* so freely glide.
To what name do you answer?
I am called Beeba.
This is my servant, Gwum...
...though weak of mind, his heart is true enough.
Am I not mistaken to assume that you, like my tribe, are on a pilgrimmage to yonder shrine, where lies the buried *Amnolia*?
It is as you have forseen, Great Chieftain.
You would do better to come with us, my friends, for the road is as rough as it is long and steep.
I fear that so great an honor is beyond our capacity to bear, Mighty Chieftain...
...for we possess nothing with which to repay such lavish generosity.
Nonsense! My guards will show you to your rooms at once.
So it was that a few deftly quoted passages from *The Hemmin Spotter* provided us with several nights of free room and board, not to mention a **very** unique means of transportation.
Not bad, eh, Gwum?

We're not out of this yet, Bobo. Fast talk and fancy words can only take you so far.
Hm! You've turned out to be a real *party pooper*, you know that, Gwum?
That night, as Gwum and I lay sleeping, an alarm was sounded throughout the fortress.
LANG
LANG
LANG
What is it, men?
**Charklugs,** sir!
They've surrounded the fortress...
...**hundreds** of them!
By the time Gwum and I had gotten up to see what was going on, the entire fortress was under siege!
Roooooooooo

Chieftain Mordloff marshalled his troops in defense of the fortress. Shouting orders to one man after another, he soon had the entire tribe positioned for a counterattack.
Lieutenant Grondo! Take your men to the rear!
Not a single Churklug is to be allowed aboard this fortress!
His men employed an impressive array of weaponry, including whirling blades and barrels of scalding hot oil.
Though superior in numbers, the Churklugs were suffering horrendous casualties.

The battle raged on through the night. By daybreak, Mordloff's men had proven victorious, and the Churklugs were driven into a hasty and ignominious retreat.
As the last of them limped off into the shadows, we descended from the fortress to survey the carnage.
Human life was not meant to be so senselessly squandered.
"Truly it is madness unbridled, whenever men take up arms against one another."
Forgive my ignorance, Great Chieftain, but who are these Churklugs, and what grievance do they hold against your tribe?
It has always been thus, and to this day unquestioned it remains, that Churklugs, as men of the land, resent and oppose the movement of nomads such as I.
And yet we wish not to provoke their fury, only to pass unhindered through their land so that we might complete our pilgrimmage to the Amnolia Shrine.
To follow a road so perilous you are brave indeed, Great Chieftain. Your desire to read that buried manuscript must be even more fervent than my own.
In a flash, Mordloff turned on me!
READ?
READ?!!

SHIK
THWUMP
FFFFFF
It is forbidden that anyone...
...ANYONE...
...should read the last chapter of The Hemmin Spotter!
It is?
I mean it is!
Of course it is! H-how could it be otherwise?!
Mordloff's eyes were twitching like a man possessed. I had no doubt that he intended to kill me right there on the spot.
Finally, though, his face softened and he pulled back.
Forgive me, friend.
The Churklug attack has strained my nerves.
Surely my ears were playing tricks on me...
...for you couldn't possibly have said what I thought you said.

And so I came to realize that Mordloff's attitude towards *The Hemmin Spotter* was radically different from my own, though no less obsessive.
Come then. Many miles yet remain between us and our destination.
Back aboard the moving fortress, Gwum and I discussed the matter in private.
He's off his rocker, this fellow! His reverence for the book is understandable, but he's treating the missing text as if it were some sort of sacred relic!
He's a nut case, all right. I say we get off this thing as soon as we can and head back to Malbadoo.
Don't be ridiculous, Gwum. Nothing could look more suspicious!
I'm afraid we're going to have to see this thing through now that we've come this far.
And since old Mordloff won't let anyone get a look at that buried manuscript, I've little choice but to sneak into the Shrine and dig it up in the middle of the night.
Have you lost your mind?! You nearly got a dagger up your nose for just **talking** about getting your hands on that thing!
Gwum, you don't know what's at **stake** here...
And **you** don't know when to leave well enough **alone!**
Come on, Bobo: Whirling blades! Scalding oil! These people don't just **inflict** pain, they get **into** it!
I don't care **how** much money this thing is worth...

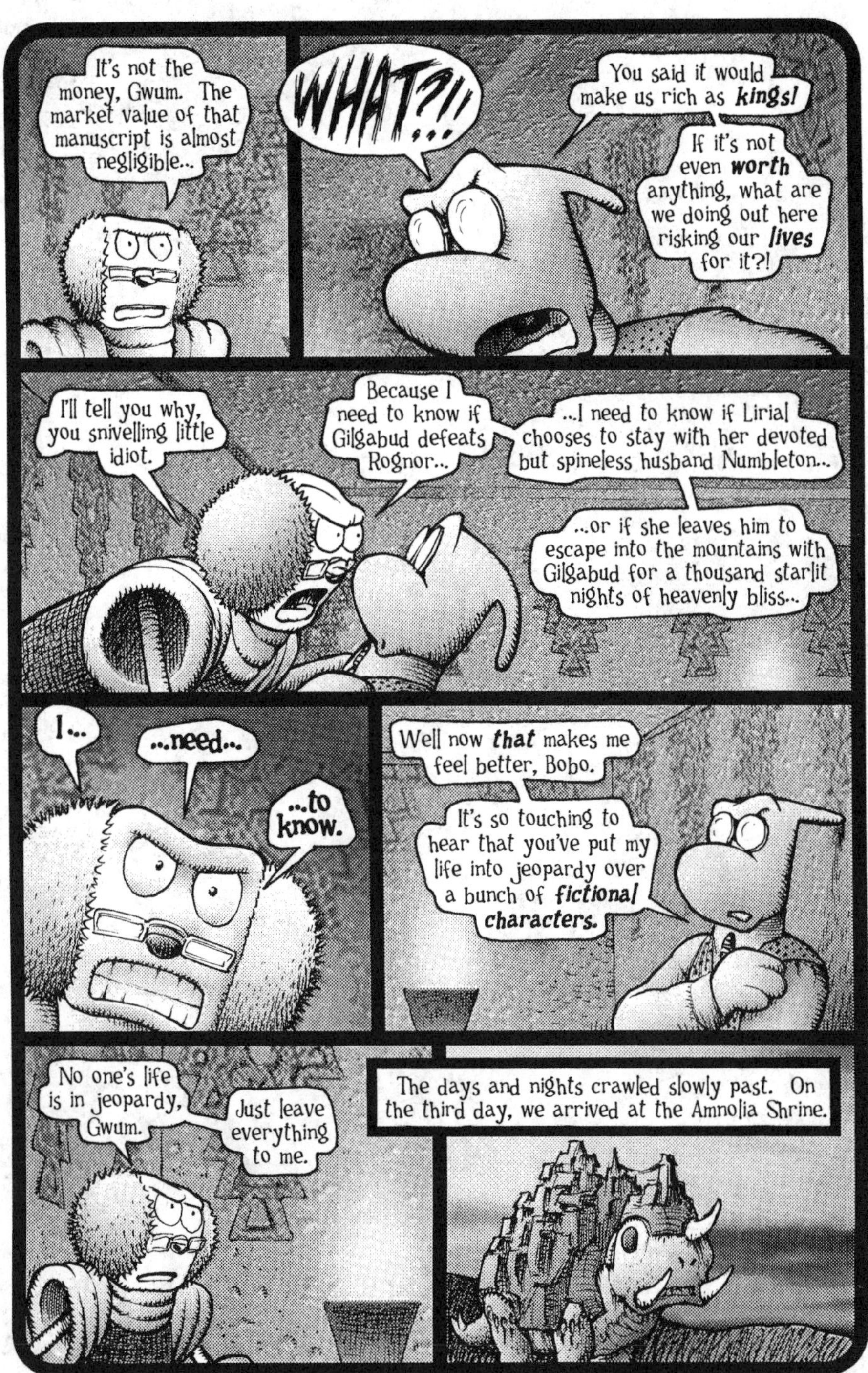
It's not the money, Gwum. The market value of that manuscript is almost negligible...
WHAT?!!...
You said it would make us rich as **kings!**
If it's not even **worth** anything, what are we doing out here risking our **lives** for it?!
I'll tell you why, you snivelling little idiot.
Because I need to know if Gilgabud defeats Rognor...
...I need to know if Lirial chooses to stay with her devoted but spineless husband Numbleton...
...or if she leaves him to escape into the mountains with Gilgabud for a thousand starlit nights of heavenly bliss...
I...
...need...
...to know.
Well now **that** makes me feel better, Bobo.
It's so touching to hear that you've put my life into jeopardy over a bunch of **fictional characters.**
No one's life is in jeopardy, Gwum.
Just leave everything to me.
The days and nights crawled slowly past. On the third day, we arrived at the Amnolia Shrine.

Mordloff called his top men together for a late night meeting in front of the Shrine.

This year an added pleasure we will enjoy.

I am inviting my new friend, Beeba, to take part in tomorrow's ceremony.

Mighty Chieftain, it is too great an honor...

Your modesty is excessive, friend.

There is none among us able to recite *The Hemmin Spotter* so flawlessly as you.

Rest well and sleep deeply this night...

...for the ceremony tomorrow will require all the stamina you can muster.

So did you dig up the manuscript in the middle of the night?

I'm ***getting*** to that, Akiko. Have patience.

Poog says to skip all the yakkity-yak and bring on the action!

I appreciate your sudden desire to enter the field of ***simultaneous translation,*** Spuckler, but Poog said nothing of the sort.

He simply reminded me to tell you about Gwum's "little secret."

Hmm... The plot thickens, eh?
It gets very thick indeed, Akiko. Trust me.
So what was he keeping from you?
Let's just say that my bookish friend Gwum was not all that he appeared to be...
That night, after Mordloff and his men had gone to sleep, Gwum and I made preparations for my "midnight excavation."
I can't believe you're actually going **through** with this, Bobo.
You should come *with* me, Gwum. There's nothing like the thrill of discovering great literature!
I wonder how **thrilled** Mordloff will be when he discovers you've made off with his sacred manuscript!
I'm not **making off** with anything, Gwum.
I'm simply going to dig it up, read it, and bury it again.
What if it's poorly written? For all you know it could be total **schmaltz** at the end!
I suppose that's just a risk I'll have to take, isn't it?
I can hear you now...
"Oh Gwum, what a letdown! Rognor beat the living daylights out of my hero, Gilgabird!"
Gilga**bud.**
Honestly, Gwum. It's as if you'd never read a book in your life!

And what if I **hadn't?** Would that make me any less of a **person?!**
Gwum, just what is it you're trying to tell me?
Look, it's not **my** fault I never learned how to read!
I had...
...very uninspirational teachers!
Never...
...learned how to **read?**
The glasses. The necktie.
It's all just a clever disguise!
No **wonder** you failed the Virpluck exam!
I scored surprisingly well on the multiple choice, actually.
Gwum, old friend, you should have told me this **ages** ago.
I'd be **happy** to teach you how to read!
You...
...you would?
It will be the first thing I do once we get back to the university!
And with that, I began my covert operation to dig up and read the last chapter of *The Hemmin Spotter.*
**Do** be careful, Bobo!
I could get **killed** out here tonight, Gwum...
...the least you could do is stop calling me "Bobo."

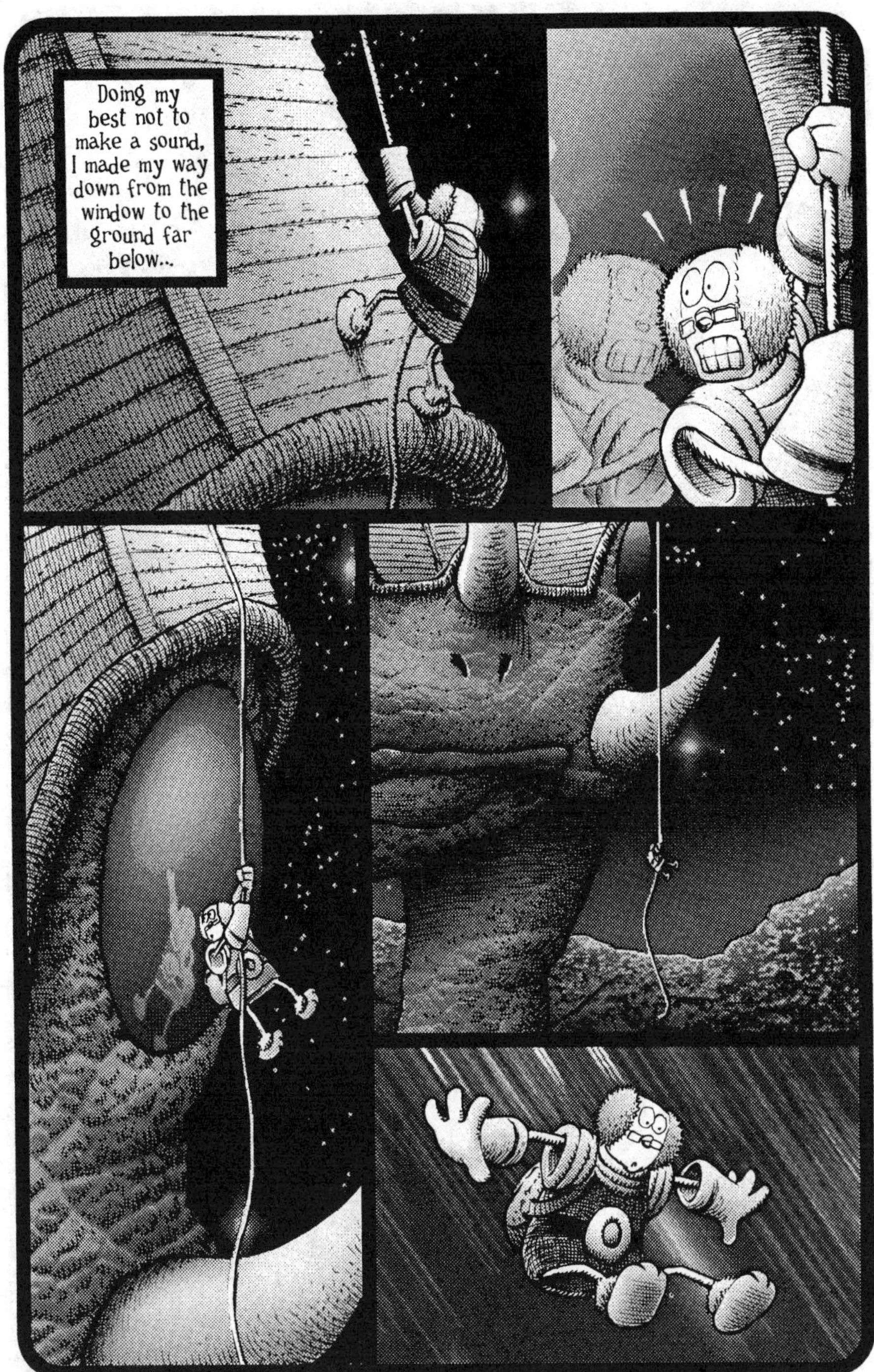
Doing my best not to make a sound, I made my way down from the window to the ground far below...

KLIK
FRAW

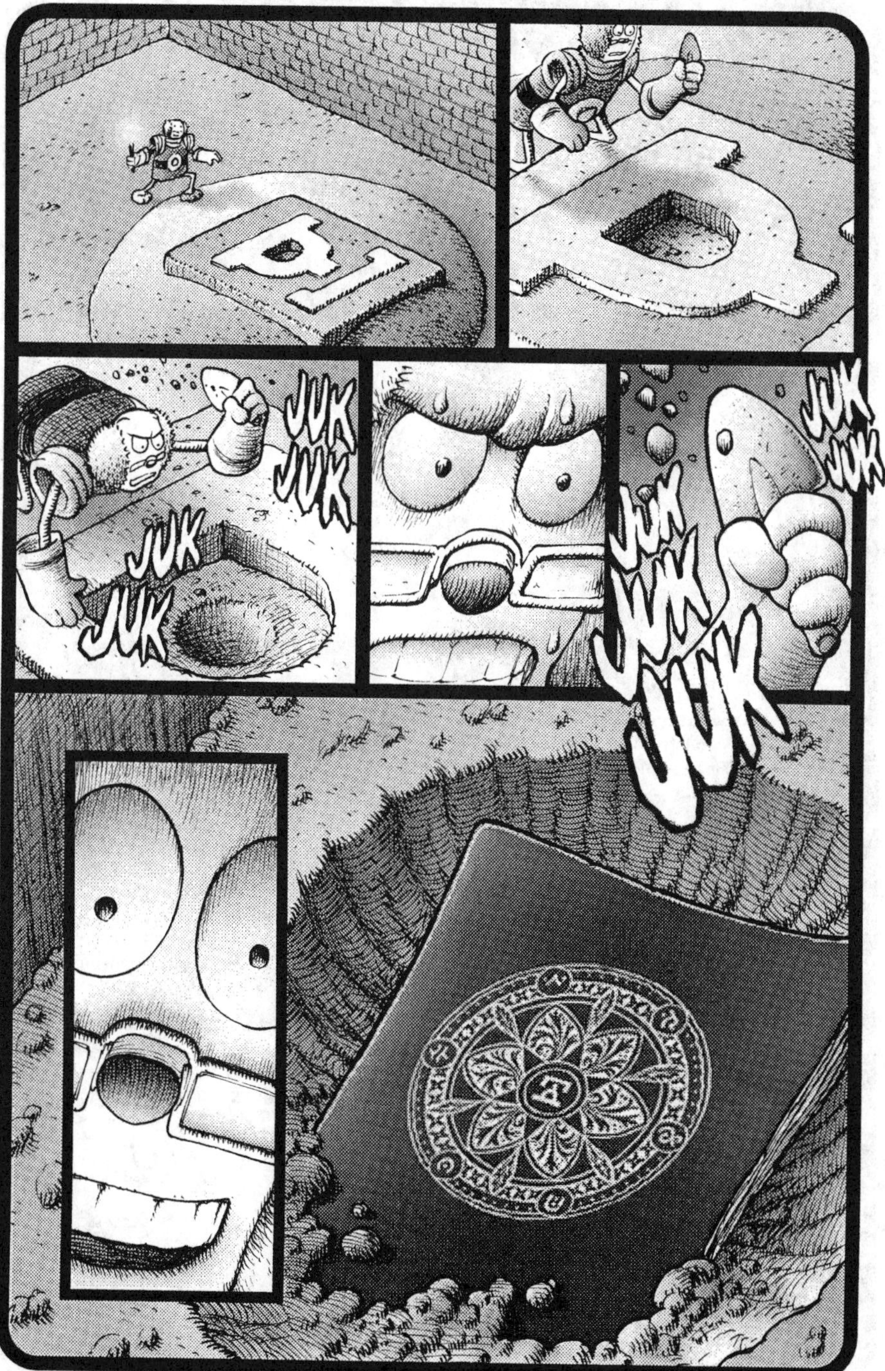
JUK
JUK
JUK
JUK
JUK
JUK
JUK
JUK
JUK

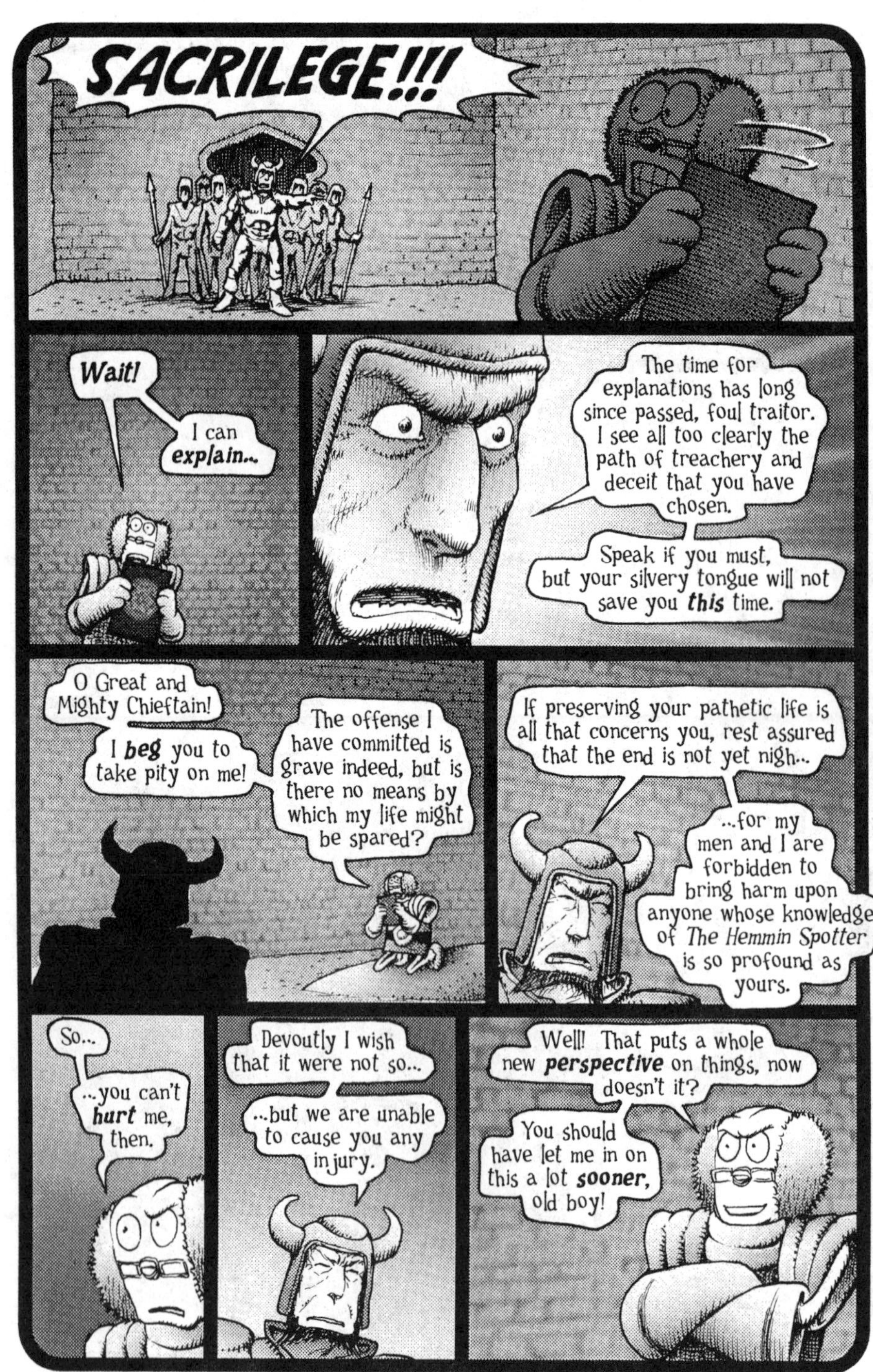
SACRILEGE!!!
Wait!
I can explain...
The time for explanations has long since passed, foul traitor. I see all too clearly the path of treachery and deceit that you have chosen.
Speak if you must, but your silvery tongue will not save you this time.
O Great and Mighty Chieftain!
I beg you to take pity on me!
The offense I have committed is grave indeed, but is there no means by which my life might be spared?
If preserving your pathetic life is all that concerns you, rest assured that the end is not yet nigh...
...for my men and I are forbidden to bring harm upon anyone whose knowledge of The Hemmin Spotter is so profound as yours.
So...
...you can't hurt me, then.
Devoutly I wish that it were not so...
...but we are unable to cause you any injury.
Well! That puts a whole new perspective on things, now doesn't it?
You should have let me in on this a lot sooner, old boy!

I advise you not to abuse your privileged status!
I didn't **ask** for your advice.
Now if you don't mind, I've got a bit of **reading** to catch up on...
NO!!
If you read so much as a **word** of that manuscript, there will be dire consequences!
Ooooh, you're **threatening** me, aren't you?
What are you going to do, call me names?
You leave me no other choice.
Keep it down, will you, Chief?
I've read the same sentence **five times** since you barged in here...
Men! Bring in the captive!
"Captive?"
Only then did I realize that Mordloff had **other** means of persuasion at his disposal...
Come on, Bobo...
...stop reading that thing and hand it over to them!
You would do well to heed the words of your friend...
...for there is no rule that prevents me from injuring **him.**
But...
...but **he** knows as much about *The Hemmin Spotter* as ***I*** do!
He's a scholar!
He's a ***simpleton!***
He knows not even the name of the main character!

Sorry, Bobo...
...they tested me.
Clearly the poor fellow is suffering from amnesia...
Enough of your lies!
SHING
Give me the book or I will kill your friend right here and now!
I've got a better idea: I'll just sort of skim over it really quickly...
...and you let him off with a minor flesh wound!
No compromises!
Hand me the manuscript...
...or watch your friend die.
Beeba...
...Beeba, please...

Go on.
Take it.
Quickly! Before I change my mind...
For once you have chosen wisely.
Light a fire, men...
...we shall burn the text immediately!
What?!
Have you gone insane?!
It is an ironclad rule of our tribe: once a man has tainted the sacred Amnolia by laying his hands upon it, the text must be destroyed to prevent further desecrations.
I was wearing gloves!
It makes no difference.
WHERE DO YOU GET THESE RULES?!!!...
I think you're making them up as you go along!!
Silence!
That will do nicely, men.
Step aside.
Stop and think about what you're doing here! If you burn that manuscript, no one will ever know how The Hemmin Spotter ends!
And so it was intended to be.
Strange, that a man so educated as you should fail to grasp this simple truth.

And with that, Mordloff tossed the book onto the fire.
I watched helplessly as it curled in upon itself...
...and disappeared into the flames.
When the rest of the tribe learns what has happened, their rage will be such that I cannot guarantee your safety.
I urge you to leave us at once.
Trust me, Mordloff...
...there is no longer **any** reason for us to stay here!
Bidding our eccentric hosts farewell, Gwum and I began the long and tiresome trek back to the University of Malbadoo.
I was so close, Gwum...
...so **close!**
You know, I think he **was** making up the rules as he went along...
...you're just lucky he came up with one that saved **your** skin!
Stop looking on the bright side, will you, Gwum?
I **hate** it when people do that!

So did you teach Gwum how to read?
Oh yes, Akiko. He was quite a *voracious* reader by the time I was done with him.
He even went on to become a professor of literature, and a pretty good one at that!
I'll tell ya whatcha **should've** done. Ya shoulda jumped up on old Mordloff, wrestled the knife away, and then held him hostage while ya finished readin' the book!
But of course. How *silly* of me.
Makes for a better **ending,** anyway.
Well, I hope you at least **learned** something from the experience.
I did indeed, Akiko...
...if you're ever planning to go on a quest, don't bring any friends along, because your enemies will end up using them against you!
I think you need to work on your **morals,** Mr. Beeba.
You know, Spuckler, maybe you're right.
I probably **could** have gotten that knife away from Mordloff if I tried...
Maybe.
I kind of doubt it, though...
..."Bobo."
All right, this is going to stop **right now.**
"Bobo."
**Shut up!**
"Bobo."
Give me a hand here, Akiko. I'm sure we can give him an awfully good tickling between the ***two*** of us...
The End

I don't know about the rest of you guys, but I'm ready for another story!
Why don't you tell us about your exploits on the planet Brunk, Spuckler?
A rather thrilling yarn, as I recall...
Yeah, I got myself into a real mess *that* time, didn't I?
IT'S A WONDER YOU LIVED TO TELL THE TALE, SIR.
C'mon, let's hear it!
Now hang on a second, 'Kiko. I gotta decide where to start.
What's to decide? Begin at the beginning!
Well, now it ain't that simple.
There's more than one way to tell a story, y' know...
You can start out at the beginning like you say, an' go through the history an all that junk so as everyone'll know what's goin' on...
...or else you can jump right on into the exciting stuff an' just let everybody sink or swim!
I think I already know which way *you* prefer.
Get ready to swim, folks!

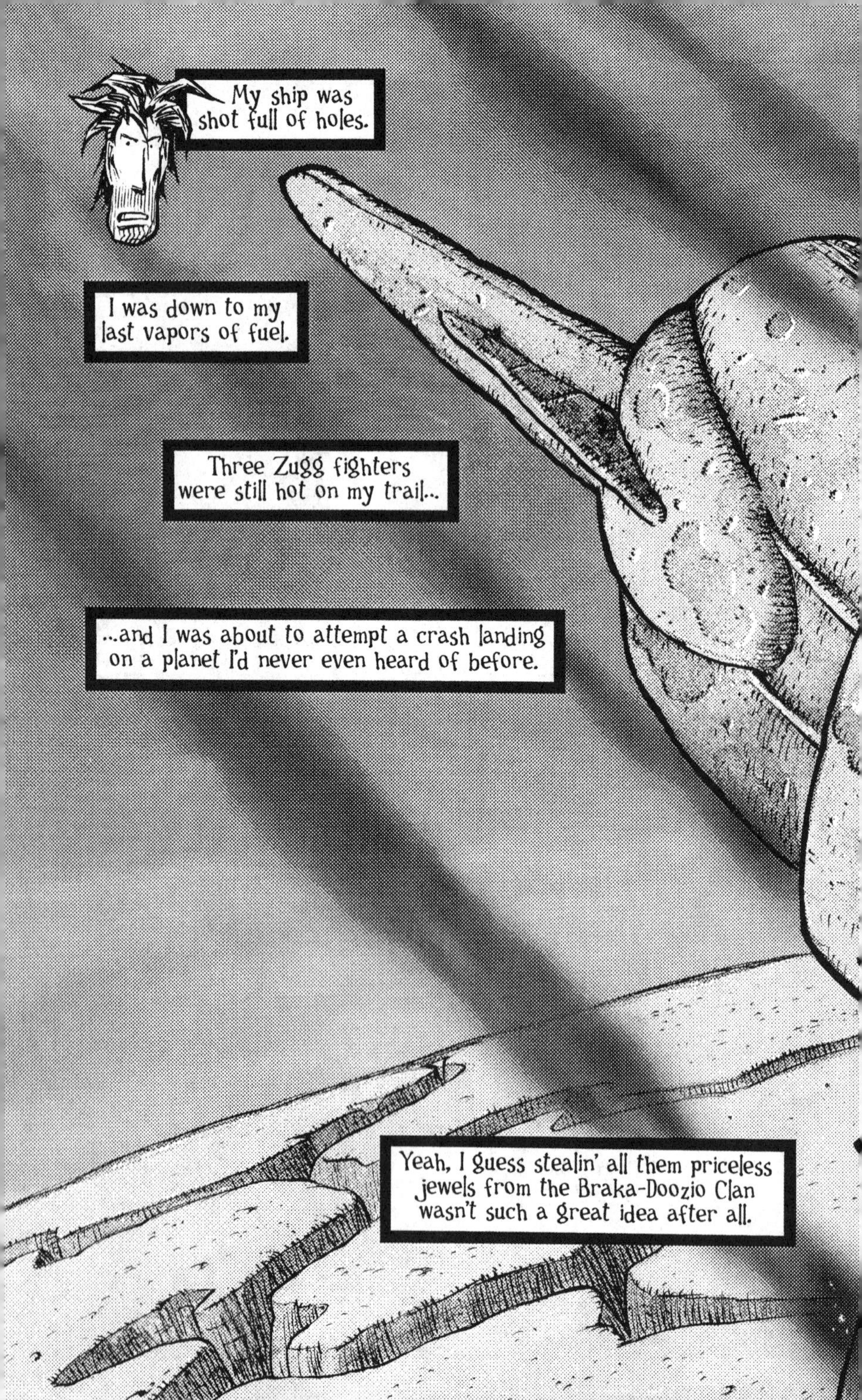
My ship was shot full of holes.
I was down to my last vapors of fuel.
Three Zugg fighters were still hot on my trail...
...and I was about to attempt a crash landing on a planet I'd never even heard of before.
Yeah, I guess stealin' all them priceless jewels from the Braka-Doozio Clan wasn't such a great idea after all.

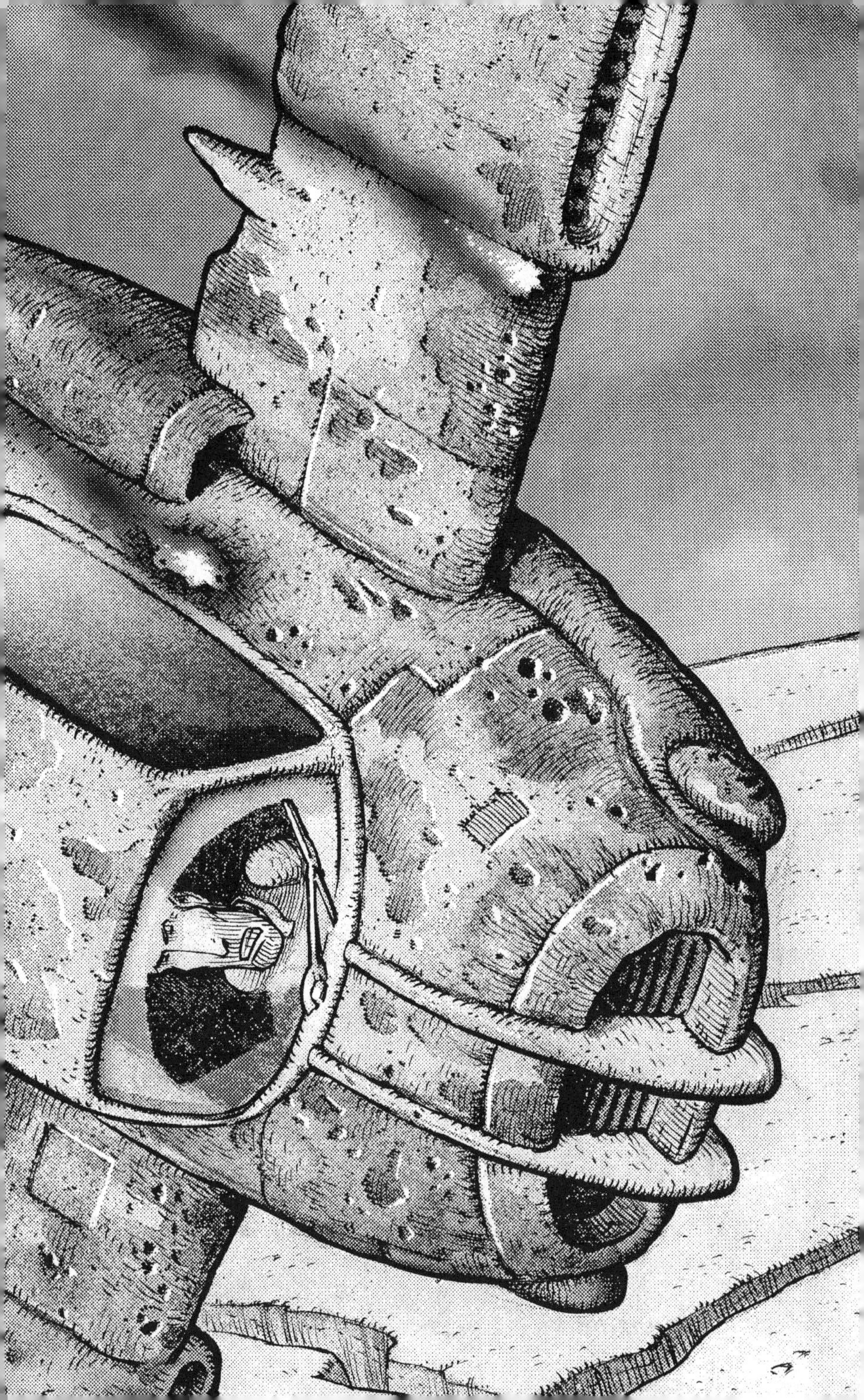

The Zuggs were closin' in fast. There was only one way out...
...the old "turn-sideways-and-fly-through-the-crack-in-the-mountain" trick.
Risky? Sure...
...but you know me: I *live* for that kinda stuff.
All right, Buddy boys...
...let's see if you're as dumb as I **think** you are.

FLAM
FLAM
FLAM
Yeeeeee-
-HAAAAW!!!
Dang.
Out of juice...
...and not a gas station in sight.

C'mon, Spuck...
...nice n' easy, now...
....just like Daddy taught'cha...
FOOOOOOOOOOOOOM
The ship came to a stop right smack dab in the middle of nowhere. I got out and had a look around.
K'CHOK
There wasn't much to see, though.
No gas.
No food.
No water.
Some planet **this** turned out to be.
The sun was hot enough to cook a man inside of five minutes.
I crawled back inside the ship for a little shuteye.
Reclinin' seats...
**...that's** what this ship needs.
ZZZZZ

HEY YOU!
Out of the ship!
Now!
Whoever it was, they had a pretty big gun.
I figured I'd better play along.
Who sent you?
Nobody sent me. I came here on my own...
...and I'm kinda startin' to ***regret*** it if you really wanna know the truth.
Show me your landing permit.
I ain't ***got*** no landing permit.
When there's a bunch of Zugg fighters gunnin' at ya, takin' care of paperwork ain't exactly the first thing on your mind, pal.
But... but ***no*** one comes to the planet Brunk without prior authorization from the Kortok!
Look, I picked this planet mainly 'cause I was runnin' outta fuel, and if all the locals are as friendly as ***you*** are, then I ain't gonna be stayin' here very long.
So why don't ya just put the gun away for a second...
...and take your mask off so as we can talk this thing over, man to man?
I don't think we'll be doing ***that***...

For heaven's sake wipe that moronic expression off your face!
It's as if you'd never seen a **woman** before.
I...
...I ain't never seen one that looked like ***you.***
Flattery will get you ***nowhere,*** mystery man.
Now I don't know where you came from or where you're going, but we've got to get out of here before the ***surveillance patrols*** see us.
What about my ship?
What ***about*** it?
We can't just ***leave*** it here!
Well unless you can pick it up and carry it on your shoulder, I don't see that we have much ***choice!***
But ***look*** at her!
Ain't ya got a ***heart?***
Listen to me. You don't know what kind of planet you've ***landed*** on here.
You're an ***illegal entry...***
...and if they catch you they'll imprison you for ***life!***

I had no idea who "they" were, but she looked so scared I figured I'd better save the questions for later.
She led me to a light transport glider she'd hidden behind some rocks.
I hope this thing is sturdier than it *looks.*
It's more than strong enough for the two of us.
My grandfather built it *himself.*
I take it that's supposed to put my mind at ease.
My grandfather is a *genius.*
If he's so smart...
...why'd he forgot to build a *backseat?!*

I'll tell ya **one** thing. She was a heckuva a good pilot with that old glider. She took it through places even *I* wouldn't have tried.
At first I thought she was just showin' off, but then I realized she was makin' sure we weren't bein' followed by nobody.
A coupla minutes later we arrived at her "secret hideout

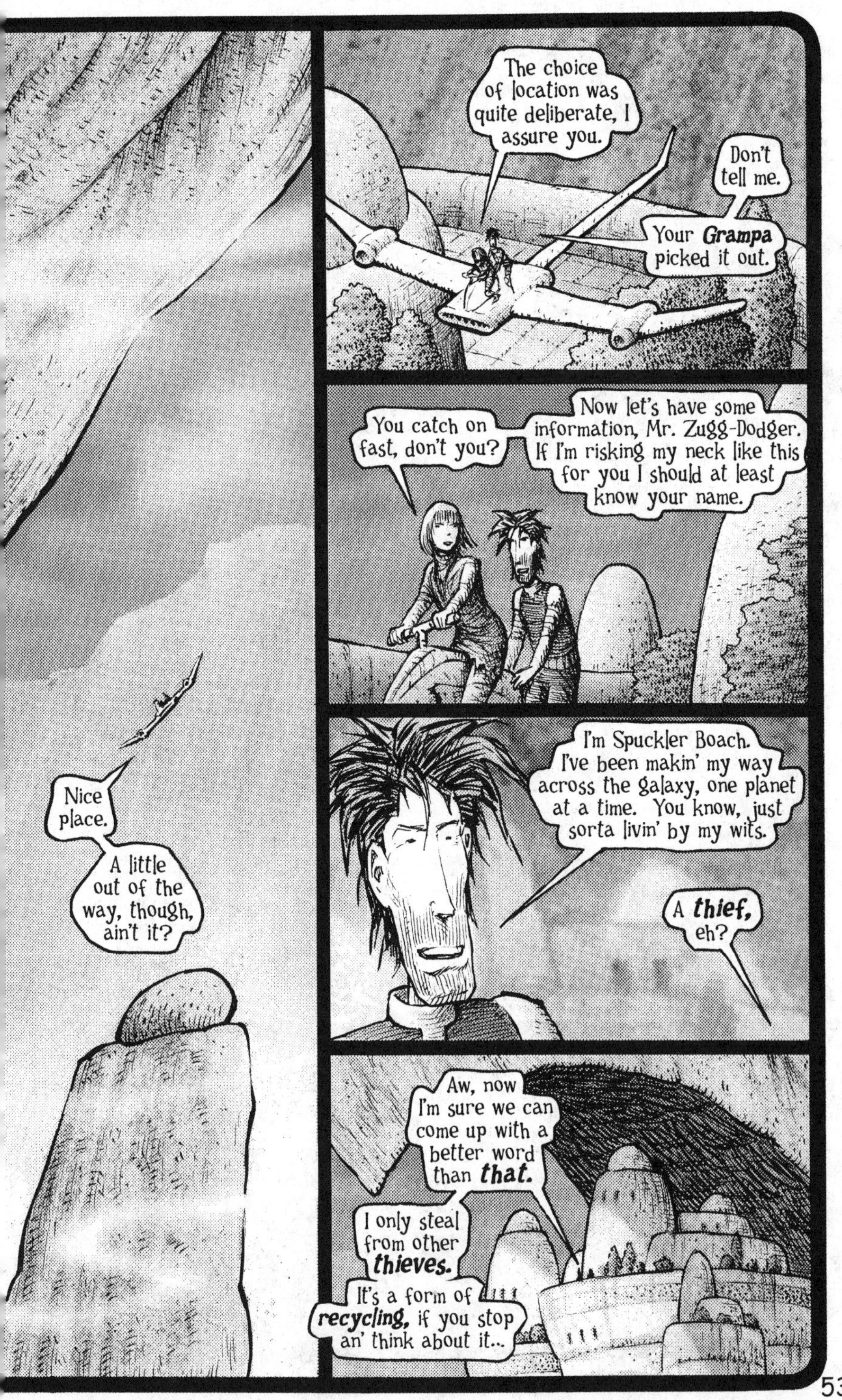
Nice place.
A little out of the way, though, ain't it?
The choice of location was quite deliberate, I assure you.
Don't tell me.
Your **Grampa** picked it out.
You catch on fast, don't you?
Now let's have some information, Mr. Zugg-Dodger. If I'm risking my neck like this for you I should at least know your name.
I'm Spuckler Boach. I've been makin' my way across the galaxy, one planet at a time. You know, just sorta livin' by my wits.
A **thief,** eh?
Aw, now I'm sure we can come up with a better word than **that.**
I only steal from other **thieves.**
It's a form of **recycling,** if you stop an' think about it...

No **wonder** you had Zugg fighters on your tail. Who sent them after you?
The Braka-Doozio Clan. They hired me to transport some stolen jewels...
...I kinda got lost along the way.
Well, you'll be safe **here.**
Even the **Kortok** doesn't know about this place.
Y' know, you got a nasty habit of throwin' that word around like everybody knows what it **means.**
The Kortok? It's an alliance of warlords that's ruled this planet for centuries.
They keep us under their control by monitoring us at every turn.
Whaddya mean, "us?"
Sounds to me like you're pretty much off the **map** s'far as these Kortok fellers are concerned.
You're right. **My** life is free enough...
...but only because of my grandfather's sacrifice. He hid me here before he was sent to prison.
Prison? What did he do?
**Nothing!**
His only crime was being a popular local leader.
People loved him so much the Kortok considered him a threat to their authority.
That's wrong.
It's jus' plain, old **wrong.**
It's best not to talk about it.
You got **that** right. It's time to stop talkin', and **do** somethin' about it!
Like **what?**
You just leave that to me.

Wow, Spuckler...
...you didn't tell us this was going to be a love story!
Now hang on a second, 'Kiko, you're gettin' the wrong idea. I was just helpin' her out 'cause it was the right thing to do, that's all.
Yeah, right.
Poog agrees with Akiko. He thinks you were head over heels for her!
Poog didn't say that!
It was a loose translation, I'll admit.
Look, Spuckler, there's nothing wrong with having a little crush on someone, is there?
Maybe you did it because you liked her and because it was the right thing to do.
All right, all right!
If I admit I liked her, will ya let me get on with it?!
Of course, Spuckler.
Just promise you'll tell us if you kissed her.
You guys really know how to ruin a good story, you know that?

It took some persuadin', but she finally agreed to let me try'n break her Grampa out of jail.
I had her fly me to the outskirts of the nearest city, a gambling town called Mull Garoon.
All right.
This'll be close enough.
Now remember your end of the bargain...
Stop worrying about your little spaceship, Mr. Boach. I'll have it patched up by the time you get back.
Just one more thing.
What?
If I'm gonna risk my neck like this for ya...
...I should at least know your name.
Muna.
Muna.
That's pretty.
Keep your mind on the *plan*, Boach.
The plan...
Well, I didn't really ***have*** a plan, to tell ya the truth.
That's the problem with bein' a hero: most of the time ya just have to wing it.

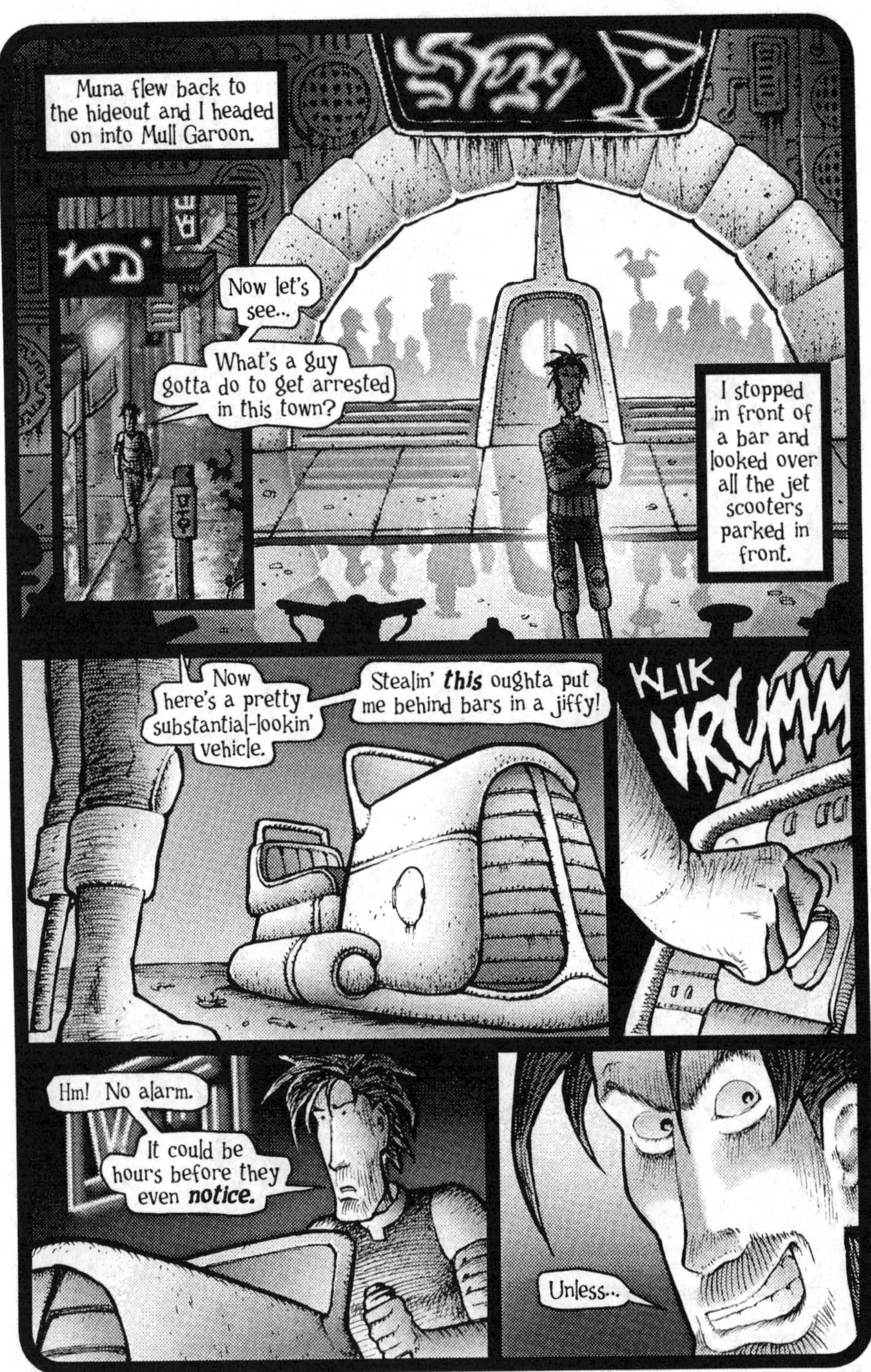
Muna flew back to the hideout and I headed on into Mull Garoon.
Now let's see...
What's a guy gotta do to get arrested in this town?
I stopped in front of a bar and looked over all the jet scooters parked in front.
Now here's a pretty substantial-lookin' vehicle.
Stealin' *this* oughta put me behind bars in a jiffy!
KLIK
VRUMM
Hm! No alarm.
It could be hours before they even *notice.*
Unless...

See that lady over there, with the tentacles? She's in here every night of the **week,** I swear...
ZLURP
I'm tellin' ya, Meebo, we gotta find another hangout.
Nothin' ever **happens** in this joint...
KRAASH
Wa-
-HOOOO!!!
Well, ***that*** did the trick.
Before long there were troopers after me by the dozen!

I wanted to make good n' sure they'd toss me in the slammer, so I left my mark on a few places around town.
THASH
KOSH
The only problem was they were so dang **slow.** I had to cool my jets a coupla times or else they'd have never **caught** me.
My **Gramma** flies faster than these guys!
Finally I had to shoot into a dead-end alley just t' make it easy on 'em.
SKREEEEET
By the authority of the Kortok you are hereby placed under arrest for violation of Civil Code 17-44 and multiple infractions against Transport Rules 28-A and 28-B. If you wish to have your rights read aloud to you in full, signal by nodding your head and dismounting the vehicle.
Yeah, yeah, yeah. Jus' cuff me and cart me off to **jail** already.

I'll tell ya, these Kortok guys sure loved their **rules.** The head trooper must've spent half an hour just tellin' me what I did wrong.
All right, ya made your point: I broke the **law.**
Now are ya gonna lock me up or not?
Yours is not an imprisonable offense. You will be held at the detention center in Mull Garoon until further notice.
Hey c'mon, I just took out a coupla **buildings** back there!
What kind of namby-pamby police state **is** this?
Code 17-44 specifies that vehicular theft is to be dealt with at the regional level.
Now come along...
I had to think fast. Muna's Grampa was in a prison on one of Brunk's **moons.** Doin' time in the local detention center just wasn't gonna cut it.
I can't believe you ain't even gonna **cuff** me!
Unauthorized restraint of suspects is a violation of Code 35-11...
That's when I made my move...
FWUT
CRZAAAAT
BOAM

All right, Chief, what's your rulebook say about **that?!**
Turns out the ship I blew up belonged to the head trooper himself.
Do I know how to pick 'em or **what?**
He ordered me cuffed and chained until a heavily-armored transport cruiser could be called to the scene.
Before long they were takin' me right where I wanted to go: the maximum-security prison of Grumborg...

As the transport ship got further from Brunk, I had a feeling we were leavin' the planet behind in more ways than one.
All right, prisoner...
...on your feet!
THWAK
NGH!
Hey, take it **easy,** pal!
Ain't ya got no rules against brutality?
Oh yes, prisoner. We've got **plenty** of rules.
The thing is, you're not **on** the planet **Brunk** anymore.
You're headed to Grumborg Prison, where there's only **one** rule: Fight...
...or **die.**

Whoever built Grumborg Prison came up with a real humdinger of a design.

From the looks of it, all they did was take the biggest canyon they could find and seal it over with a roof of solid steel.

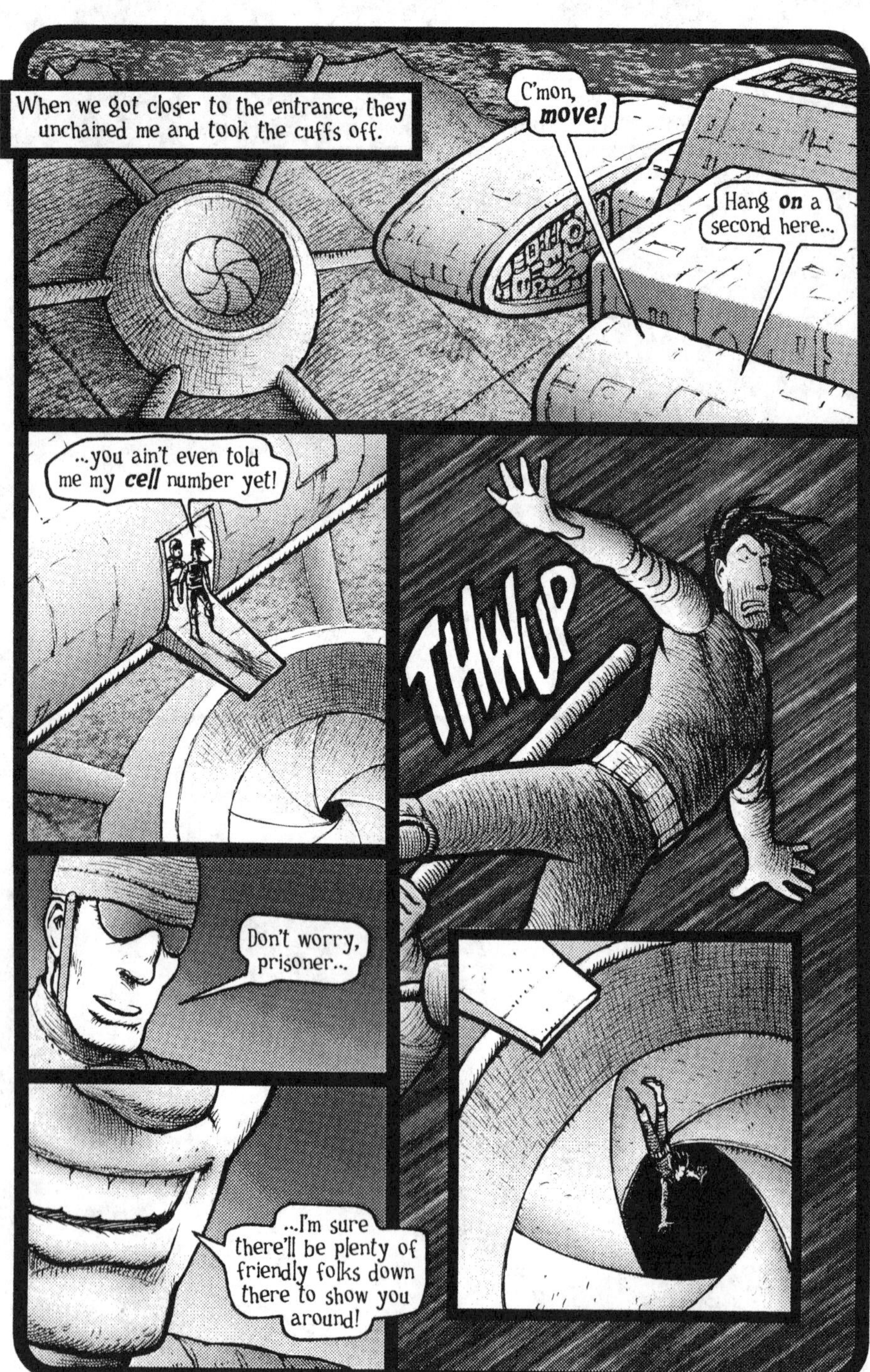

When we got closer to the entrance, they unchained me and took the cuffs off.
C'mon, **move!**
Hang **on** a second here...
...you ain't even told me my ***cell*** number yet!
THWUP
Don't worry, prisoner...
...I'm sure there'll be plenty of friendly folks down there to show you around!

FOOOOOOOING
OPEN IT UP!!! OPEN IT UP!!!
Hey c'mon, squibb-for-brains, we're *starvin'* here!
What are you guys, blind?!
This ain't th' rations shipment, f' cryin' out loud...
...it's a new prisoner!

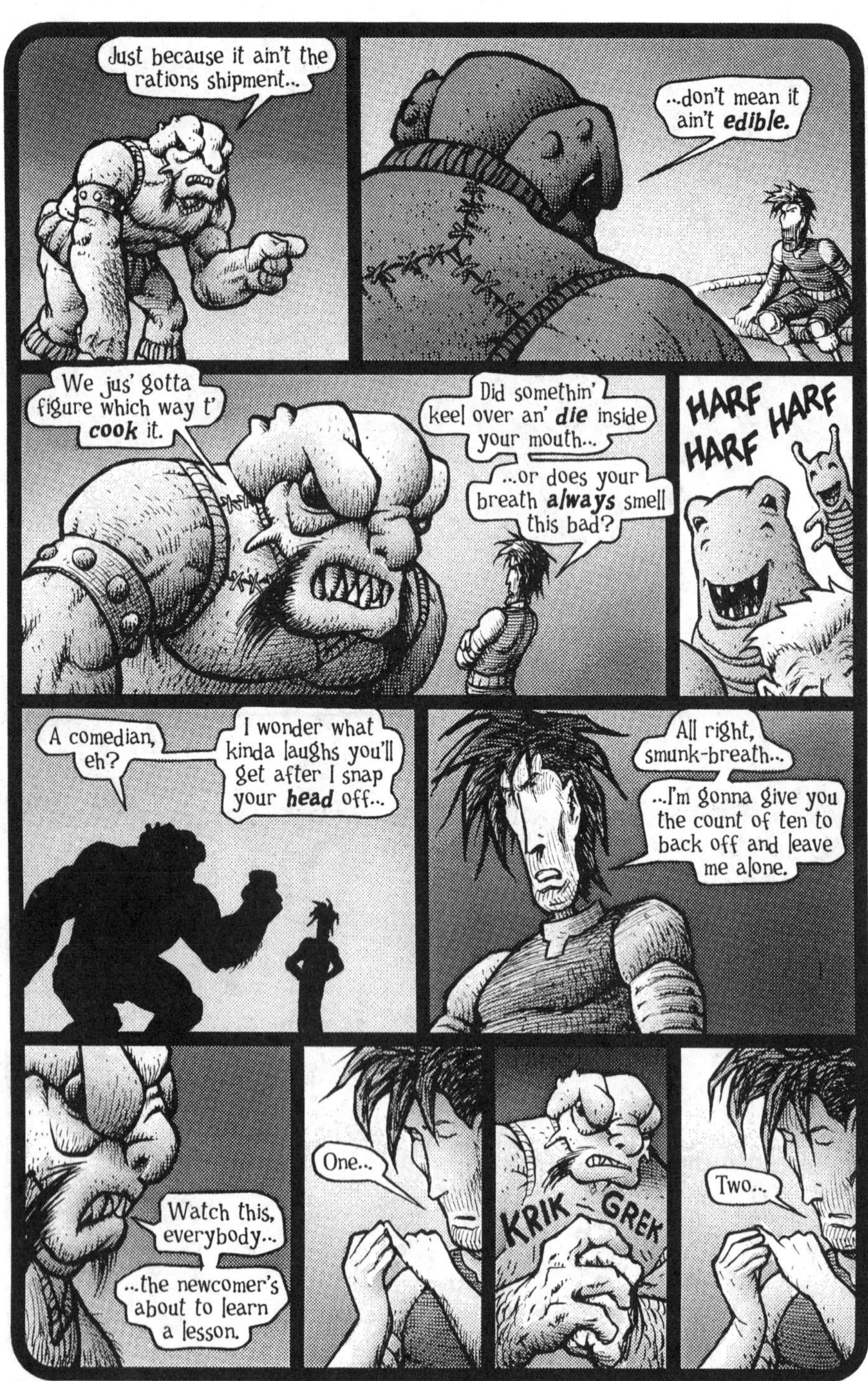
Just because it ain't the rations shipment...
...don't mean it ain't **edible.**
We jus' gotta figure which way t' **cook** it.
Did somethin' keel over an' **die** inside your mouth...
...or does your breath **always** smell this bad?
HARF HARF HARF HARF
A comedian, eh?
I wonder what kinda laughs you'll get after I snap your **head** off...
All right, smunk-breath...
...I'm gonna give you the count of ten to back off and leave me alone.
Watch this, everybody...
...the newcomer's about to learn a lesson.
One...
KRIK GREK
Two...

Aw forget it.
NGH
THUNK
THUNK
THUNK
YAAAARGH
Stop!
Stop, I say!
Stop this nonsense, **both** of you!
Aw, man...
...it was just gettin' **good.**

Dargo!
Go to your hole!
But gov'ner...
GO!!
You.
Come with me.
This guy had the respect of every thug and cutthroat in the whole joint. It didn't take me long to figure out who he was.
You're Morbilus Grendy, aren'tcha?
The same. And you?
My name's Spuckler Boach.
You're a brave man, Boach.
Most men faint dead away when they meet Dargo.
I can see why. Ain't that guy ever heard of dental hygiene?
So what brings you to this horrid place?
I'm here to help you escape, Sir.
Escape, eh? You are not the first...
...many have come to me with their lofty plans, and all have failed.
You've wasted your time, friend. There is no escaping from Grumborg Prison.
I thought you were supposed to be a **genius,** Grendy, not a **quitter.**
...least that's what your granddaughter said.
**Muna!**
You've **seen** her?
**Is she all right?**

She's fine, Grendy. But she wants you outta this jail somethin' awful.
I'd give anything...
...**anything**...
...to see my granddaughter again.
Well **you're** the guy with the brains, Grendy.
You come up with an escape plan, and I'll take care of the nuts an' bolts.
Actually, I **did** have an idea some time ago.
It's just a matter of working out the details...
Grendy led me to a cave where he said he did his best thinkin'.
Yes, of course!
Why didn't I think of this **before?!**
I don't know if ol' Grendy was a bonafide genius or not, but the plan he came up with... well, it looked pretty good on **paper**, I guess...
...when the candles melt down past a certain point, the accumulated weight of the wax droppings will cause this lever to fall, overturning the jar of ball bearings and releasing the helium balloons...
Grendy...
I know what you're thinking: what if the smoke machines fail to generate adequate cover?
No, Grendy...
You're right. But let's have a look at plan B...

GRENDY!!!
We gotta be realistic here! This plan of yours is real impressive, but it's way too complicated.
How so?
Well, let's start with the feathers. Where are we gonna find any feathers down here, let alone 300 pounds of 'em?
A pity. That was one of my favorite parts of the plan...
Trust me, Grendy. I've broken out of a lot of prisons, and I ain't never used feathers even once.
Now tell me...
...have ya ever thought of diggin' a tunnel outta here?
Of course I have. It's the first thought of anyone who gets tossed into this hole...
...but I'm afraid our captors were very wise when they chose this location.
We are surrounded on all sides by solid Pokstone.
Pokstone?
Pokstone is one of the strongest materials in the universe. It is all but impenetrable...
...ordinary picks and hammers can't even make a scratch on it.
Hmmm...
...what if we had a pick axe made of Trutanium?
Trutanium?!
Now who's being unrealistic?
Work with me here, Grendy.
Would Trutanium do the job?
Well...
...yes.
If by some miracle we had access to such a thing, we could conceivably dig through the Pokstone.
I must be some kind of miracle man, Grendy...

...'cause I just happen to have some Trutanium **on** me!
You **do?!**
Where is it?
**Show** it to me!
Have a little faith, Grendy.
**I'm** handlin' the nuts and bolts, remember?
Grendy an' me went lookin' for the best place to dig. 'Course, it didn't take a genius to figure that the higher we climbed, the less diggin' we'd have to do.
My idea about the helium balloons is starting to sound **better**, isn't it?
Keep climbin', Grendy, we're almost there...
Finally we reached a ledge just below the prison ceiling.
All right, boy. Let's see this Trutanium of yours.

You're lookin' at it.
Your peg leg?!
100% pure.
But...
...but why would anyone make a peg leg out of Trutanium?!
There are plenty of less expensive materials!
It was my Daddy's idea.
When I lost my leg, he said, "Spuck, there ain't no replacin' flesh n' bone. But I'm gonna getcha the next best thing..."
How did you lose your leg, anyway?
Well, that's a long story, Grendy. I can't tell it unless I'm in the right mood.
Now come on. We got some serious diggin' to do!
First thing I did was unscrew my peg leg.
SKREE
SKREEE
Then I set to work chippin' away at the wall.
CHAK
CHAK
Me n' Grendy worked in shifts straight through the night.
I kept tellin' Grendy about Muna, just to keep his spirits up. Funny thing, the more I talked about her, the more I started to miss her...
You should see the way she tools around with that glider you built...
...she's a real daredevil!
Heh heh! She always was a wild one, little Muna, even when she was a child!
Got us in trouble with the Kortok, of course, but I'm afraid I only encouraged her in that regard...

It took a real long time...
CHAK CHAK CHAK
...and our arms were mighty sore by the end of it...
...but finally we got to the surface.
I think these next few blows are gonna do it!
CH'HACK.
What's that smell? It's...
...delicious!
You been down here too long, Grendy.
That ain't nothin' but fresh air.
Sure enough, we'd made it outta Grumborg Prison. Now came the hard part...
...gettin' us back to the planet Brunk.
See that guard tower? I'll bet they got some transportation over there.
Don't bank on it.
As I recall, the guards in that tower rely on monthly transport freighters to get them back to Brunk.
Well, we ain't gonna git us a ride just sittin' here.
C'mon!
Keepin' low, we made our way towards the tower.
As we got closer, I saw what I was lookin' for.
Lookit, Grendy...
...up there!

Jet scooters!
Look a little closer, Boach.
There's more than just **scooters** up there.
No problem, Grendy...
...we'll just hafta work **together**, that's all.
Here's the deal: you check which scooter has the most fuel, and I'll take care of the guard.
"Take care" of him?
Don't worry, Grendy.
He'll **live.**
It was a risky plan.
The scooters were surface vehicles, an' I wasn't so sure they'd make it all the way back to Brunk in one piece.
Now, takin' care of the guard...
...that was the **fun** part.
Y'know, you really shouldn't lean back in your **chair** like that...
GRIK
...ya might get hurt.
NGH

Quickly! Before the other guards notice us!
Sorry, kid.
You're gonna be real stiff for a couple days...
I jumped in and revved up the engine.
Grendy! This tank is practically empty!
I know, I know! The others were even worse, though!
That's the problem with this star system...
...not enough gas stations.
RRRUUUUMMMM
Sure enough, we weren't even halfway to Brunk before the scooter ran out of gas.
We'll just hafta coast in on Brunk's gravity.

Coast in?! **Crash** in is more like it!
Relax, Grendy...
...things crash all the time!
Grendy was right, though. Scooters ain't built for the kinda crash we were fixin' to make, and there was a good chance we'd both end up dead as bugs on a windshield.
Unless...
I've got to hand it to you, Boach.
You've always got a trick up your sleeve...
What can I say?
Sometimes I jus' get lucky.
We landed -- surprise, surprise -- in the middle of nowhere.
Grendy said he could fly Muna's glider out to us by remote control. All he needed was the scooter's radio...

...but somehow I knew that glider wouldn't be the **only** thing flyin' in to greet us.
Grampa!
Spuckler!
Muna, dear child! Thank goodness you're okay!
Of course I'm okay!
**You're** the one who's been in prison, remember?
Ah, it wasn't so bad, really.
We are **all** prisoners of the Kortok, in one way or another.
You guys been scared of these Kortok fellers for way too long.
It's high time you chased 'em outta here and took this planet back for yourselves...
Spoken like a true revolutionary!
Perhaps you'd care to join us in the struggle?
We **need** good men like you, Boach...
Slow down, Grendy.
I ain't no revolutionary. I'm nothin' but a two-bit thief!
You are more than that, my friend...
...**much** more.
We all went back to the hideaway for some much-needed rest. Grendy ate a bellyful and fell sound asleep.
Then Muna and I went outside to enjoy a little starlight...
Grampa was **serious** about the struggle, you know...

I'm sure he was. But look at me, Muna...
...I ain't the kinda guy who gets mixed up in revolutions.
I'm used to goin' it alone.
Just because you're used to it...
...doesn't mean it's the best thing for you.
Wh-
- what's that supposed to mean?
Come on, Spuckler. Running around the galaxy, taking things as they come...
...that's fine for little boys, but don't you think it's time you settled down?
Me? Naaw...
...naw, I...
...I ain't got no plans like that.
No?
Well...
...not right now, anyway.
Think it over, Spuck...
...you might change your mind.

Well?!
Did you kiss her or not?
Use your imagination, Beebs. I ain't gonna spell everything out for ya.
Spuckler, there's nothing wrong with spelling things out, *per se*...
Just give us a hint!
So what happened after that? Did you stay and fight against the Kortok?
Well yeah, matter of fact I did. But that's a whole different story, 'Kiko. We'd best save it for another time.
Okay, but you have to promise you won't forget.
I want to hear all about this revolution you fought.
Nevermind the revolution, let's hear about that **kiss.**
Was it full on the mouth, or just a little peck on the cheek?
I ain't tellin', Beebs!
Now let it **drop**, will ya?!
It was just on the cheek, wasn't it?
The End

All right, everybody, follow me.
And watch your head. Some of these branches are pretty low.
We're almost there..
My word!
Isn't it pretty?
I call this "the Secret Place."
Nobody knows about it but me.
I dunno. 'Kiko. I was expectin' somethin' with a little more pizzazz.
I think it's perfectly lovely, Akiko.
Now whose turn is it to tell a story?
Hey Gax, you haven't told a story yet.
Do robots tell stories?
OH YES, MA'AM. SOME OF THE BEST STORYTELLERS I KNOW ARE ROBOTS, ACTUALLY.
WE'RE VERY GOOD WITH DETAILS, YOU SEE...
Well what're ya waitin' for, Gax? Spin a little yarn for us!
ARE YOU SURE, SIR? I'M AFRAID MY STORIES AREN'T VERY INTERESTING FOR NON-ANDROIDS.
They aren't.
But if ya don't hurry up, we might end up havin' to sit through another Beeba story!
WELL, SIR, IF YOU INSIST...

THIS IS THE STORY OF MY TOUR OF DUTY UPON THE FOGNON-6, THE LAST IN A SERIES OF OLD POWER STATIONS RUN BY THE GOTHTEK CORPORATION.
ONCE THE PRIDE OF ITS CREATOR, BOLTIMERE FOGNON, THE AGING FACILITY HAD FALLEN INTO A CONSTANT STATE OF DISREPAIR.
FINALLY ITS HUMAN CREW ABANDONED THE OLD STATION ALTOGETHER, LEAVING ONLY A MOTLEY ASSORTMENT OF ROBOTS BEHIND. ENSLAVED TO A TASKMASTER ROBOT BY THE NAME OF YARK, WE WERE FORCED TO WORK AROUND THE CLOCK TO KEEP THE FOGNON-6 FROM FALLING APART.

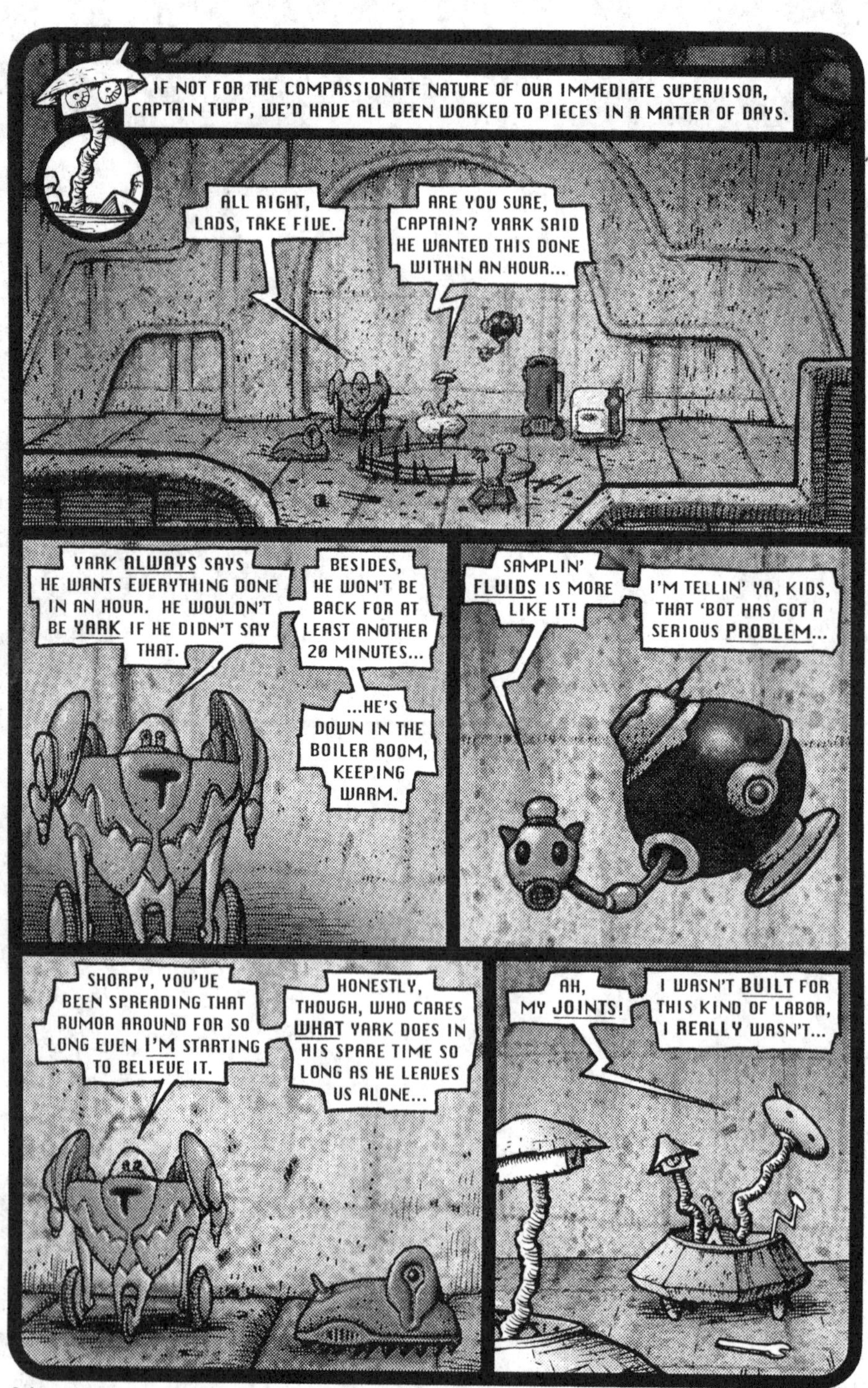
IF NOT FOR THE COMPASSIONATE NATURE OF OUR IMMEDIATE SUPERVISOR, CAPTAIN TUPP, WE'D HAVE ALL BEEN WORKED TO PIECES IN A MATTER OF DAYS.
ALL RIGHT, LADS, TAKE FIVE.
ARE YOU SURE, CAPTAIN? YARK SAID HE WANTED THIS DONE WITHIN AN HOUR...
YARK ALWAYS SAYS HE WANTS EVERYTHING DONE IN AN HOUR. HE WOULDN'T BE YARK IF HE DIDN'T SAY THAT.
BESIDES, HE WON'T BE BACK FOR AT LEAST ANOTHER 20 MINUTES...
...HE'S DOWN IN THE BOILER ROOM, KEEPING WARM.
SAMPLIN' FLUIDS IS MORE LIKE IT!
I'M TELLIN' YA, KIDS, THAT 'BOT HAS GOT A SERIOUS PROBLEM...
SHORPY, YOU'VE BEEN SPREADING THAT RUMOR AROUND FOR SO LONG EVEN I'M STARTING TO BELIEVE IT.
HONESTLY, THOUGH, WHO CARES WHAT YARK DOES IN HIS SPARE TIME SO LONG AS HE LEAVES US ALONE...
AH, MY JOINTS!
I WASN'T BUILT FOR THIS KIND OF LABOR, I REALLY WASN'T...

AND JUST WHAT EXACTLY WERE YOU BUILT FOR, GRICKS?
I'M CURIOUS.
IN OUR DAY, ROBOTS WEREN'T BUILT WITH SIMPLE FUNCTIONS IN MIND.
STYLISTIC CONCERNS WERE PARAMOUNT.
OH, I CAN SEE THAT JUST BY LOOKING AT YOU.
DIDJA COME WITH THE RUST HOLES, OR DID PEOPLE HAVE TO PAY EXTRA FOR THAT?
WE WERE THE HEIGHT OF FASHION BACK THEN, WEREN'T WE?
UNH?
OH.
OH YES, WE WERE.
MOST DEFINITELY.
WELL, I HATE TO BREAK IT TO YOU, GRIXY-BABY, BUT YOU'RE NOT STRUTTIN' DOWN THE RUNWAY ANYMORE.
WAKE UP AND SMELL THE PLETHANOL.
HEY B.B., DIDJA HEAR THAT?
I TOLD HIM TO "WAKE UP AND SMELL THE-"
AWWWW, YA GOT NO SENSE OF HUMOR.

Sounds like Shorpy and Gricks made quite a pair!
OR A THREESOME, MA'AM, DEPENDING ON HOW YOU LOOK AT IT.
Spuckler!
What on earth are you doing up there?
I'm tryin' to get a closer look at these...
...uh...
...quirrels.
Squirrels.
Are they edible?
I sure hope not.
Looks to me like they'd make a pretty good stew.
Spuckler! You're not even listening to Gax's story!
Go on without me.
I've heard this one a million times already!
So what happened next?
WELL...

...MY GREATEST FEAR WAS THAT YARK WOULD CATCH US IN THE MIDDLE OF A BREAK. ONE DAY IT FINALLY HAPPENED.
LOAFING AROUND BEHIND MY BACK!
I KNEW IT!
HE HELD CAPTAIN TUPP PERSONALLY RESPONSIBLE.
TUPP, YOU MISERABLE HEAP OF SCRAP!
PLEASE, MASTER YARK! I CAN EXPLAIN...
TRAITOR!
YOU HAVE DECEIVED ME FOR THE LAST TIME!
GRZAAAAAT
LET THIS BE A LESSON TO YOU ALL: LAZY ROBOTS GET TERMINATED.
IT'S THAT SIMPLE.
TUNK

GAX, I'M PUTTING YOU IN CHARGE AS TUPP'S REPLACEMENT.
I ADVISE YOU TO REGARD MY ORDERS WITH GREATER SERIOUSNESS THAN HE DID.
BUT MASTER YARK, I'M AN ASSISTANT ROBOT.
I WASN'T PROGRAMMED TO LEAD...
WELL, YOU'D BETTER LEARN, HADN'T YOU?
BUT MASTER YARK-
THIS IS NOT A MATTER OF DISCUSSION!
YOU WILL DO AS I SAY, OR BE DISPOSED OF LIKE YOUR PREDECESSOR.
DOES THIS MEAN WE'LL HAVE TO START CALLING HIM "CAPTAIN GAX?"
SILENCE!
BACK TO WORK, ALL OF YOU!
AND GAX...
...THERE WILL BE NO FURTHER DECEPTIONS, IS THAT CLEAR?
Y-YES, MASTER.

CIRCLING AROUND THE CHARRED REMAINS OF OUR LOST LEADER, WE CAME TO REALIZE WHAT THE FUTURE HELD IN STORE FOR US...
THE SLAVE DRIVER! HE'S GOING TO TERMINATE US ALL, ONE AT A TIME!
SHORPY'S RIGHT. YARK IS NO LONGER ACTING WITHIN THE CONFINES OF FOGNON POLICY.
THE WAY HE'S WORKING US, WE'LL ALL SHORT CIRCUIT WITHIN DAYS...
YOU NEED SPARE PARTS?!
WHAT ABOUT ME?!
I CAN'T EVEN FLY STRAIGHT ANYMORE!
WE'VE GOT TO REMAIN CALM, EVERYONE...
...CAPTAIN TUPP WOULD WANT IT THAT WAY.
LOOK, I DON'T KNOW IF YOU'VE NOTICED...
...BUT CAPTAIN TUPP IS ABOUT TEN DEGREES PAST WELL DONE RIGHT NOW.
I DON'T KNOW WHAT KIND OF CAPTAIN YOU'RE PLANNING TO BE, BUDDY, BUT WE DON'T NEED ANOTHER CAPTAIN TUPP.
WE NEED A LEADER, GAX.
SO START LEADING.

Wow. It must have been tough to handle all that pressure, Gax.
IT WASN'T EASY, MA'AM, I CAN TELL YOU THAT.
Poog says that a robot going against his programming is comparable to a sentient being going against his instincts.
I think we need an alternate translation on ***this*** one, Mr. Beeba.
I'll put it to you this way: imagine yourself in a situation where you're scared out of your wits.
Your instinct tells you to run for cover, but you resolve to hold your ground. Such a decision requires a tremendous act of will power.
Robots experience a similar struggle whenever they attempt to override their internal programming.
Is that true, Gax?
YES, MA'AM. SINCE I WAS DESIGNED TO BE AN ASSISTANT, TAKING ON THE REIGNS OF LEADERSHIP WAS A MATTER OF THE UTMOST –
GGRRAAK
FWUMP

Dang! These quirrels is the fastest li'l critters I never seen!
Spuckler! Gax sat very patiently through **your** little tale. The least you could do during **his** story is refrain from...
er...
...falling out of trees.
Carry on, Gax.

CAPTAIN TUPP'S STRATEGY OF APPEASEMENT HAD CLEARLY FAILED. I DECIDED TO PREPARE THE CREW FOR A PRE-EMPTIVE STRIKE AGAINST YARK, IN AN EFFORT TO FORCE HIM TO THE BARGAINING TABLE.

IF WE COULD SHOW HIM THAT OUR COLLECTIVE POWER WAS EQUAL TO HIS OWN, HE WOULD SURELY AGREE TO OUR MODEST DEMANDS FOR SHORTER WORKING HOURS AND MORE FREQUENT OIL CHANGES.

THOUGH NONE OF US WAS EQUIPPED WITH LETHAL WEAPONRY, WE FOUND THAT THE COMBINED STRENGTH OF OUR WELDING TOOLS COULD BE HARNASSED TO CREATE A HEAT RAY OF GREAT MAGNITUDE.

NOW YOU THREE STAY CLOSE BEHIND ME...

AND MAKE SURE THOSE CABLES REMAIN FIRMLY ATTACHED.

YES, CAPTAIN GAX.

PLEASE STOP CALLING ME THAT, GRICKS. WE ARE OLD FRIENDS, AFTER ALL.

YOU MUSN'T FORSAKE YOUR TITLE, SIR. IT'S NOT OFTEN WE ROBOTS GET PROMOTED TO SUCH A RANK, YOU KNOW...

SHORPY.

YES, YOUR MAJESTICNESS.

YOU AND B.B. KNOW WHAT DO DO WHEN WE GET THERE, RIGHT?
AYE, CAP'N!
EVERYTHING'S UNDER CONTROL.
GOOD LUCK, B.B. WE'RE ALL COUNTING ON YOU.
IT WAS TOO LATE FOR SECOND THOUGHTS. I LED THE CREW DOWN THROUGH A SERIES OF FREIGHT ELEVATORS TO YARK'S FAVORITE HIDEOUT...
..THE BOILER ROOM OF THE FOGNON 6.
AT FIRST I WAS RELIEVED TO FIND HE WASN'T THERE.
THEN I SAW HIM.

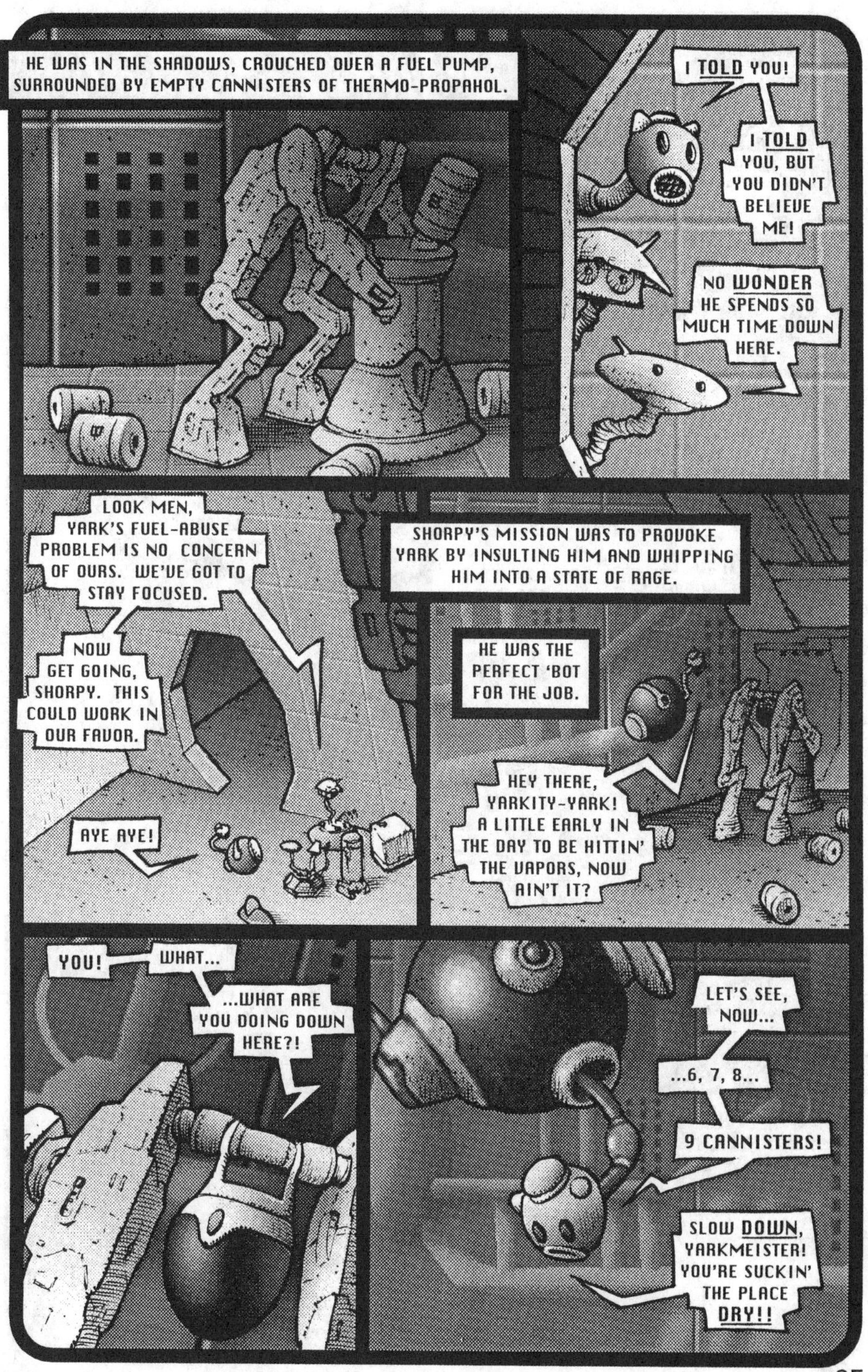

HE WAS IN THE SHADOWS, CROUCHED OVER A FUEL PUMP, SURROUNDED BY EMPTY CANNISTERS OF THERMO-PROPAHOL.
I TOLD YOU!
I TOLD YOU, BUT YOU DIDN'T BELIEVE ME!
NO WONDER HE SPENDS SO MUCH TIME DOWN HERE.
LOOK MEN, YARK'S FUEL-ABUSE PROBLEM IS NO CONCERN OF OURS. WE'VE GOT TO STAY FOCUSED.
NOW GET GOING, SHORPY. THIS COULD WORK IN OUR FAVOR.
AYE AYE!
SHORPY'S MISSION WAS TO PROVOKE YARK BY INSULTING HIM AND WHIPPING HIM INTO A STATE OF RAGE.
HE WAS THE PERFECT 'BOT FOR THE JOB.
HEY THERE, YARKITY-YARK! A LITTLE EARLY IN THE DAY TO BE HITTIN' THE VAPORS, NOW AIN'T IT?
YOU!
WHAT...
...WHAT ARE YOU DOING DOWN HERE?!
LET'S SEE, NOW...
...6, 7, 8...
9 CANNISTERS!
SLOW DOWN, YARKMEISTER! YOU'RE SUCKIN' THE PLACE DRY!!

MISERABLE WRETCH!
YOU WILL PAY FOR YOUR INSOLENCE!
GRZAAT
FASH
NOT BAD, YARKO.
FOR A GUY WHO'S AS HOPPED UP AS YOU ARE, YOU'RE STILL A PRETTY GOOD SHOT.
NOW I'D LOVE TO HANG AROUND AND HELP YOU WITH YOUR TARGET PRACTICE, BUT I'VE GOT PLACES TO GO!
COME BACK HERE, YOU LITTLE DEMON!
ALL RIGHT, B.B.
GO!
B.B. PULLED OFF HIS PART OF THE PLAN MASTERFULLY.

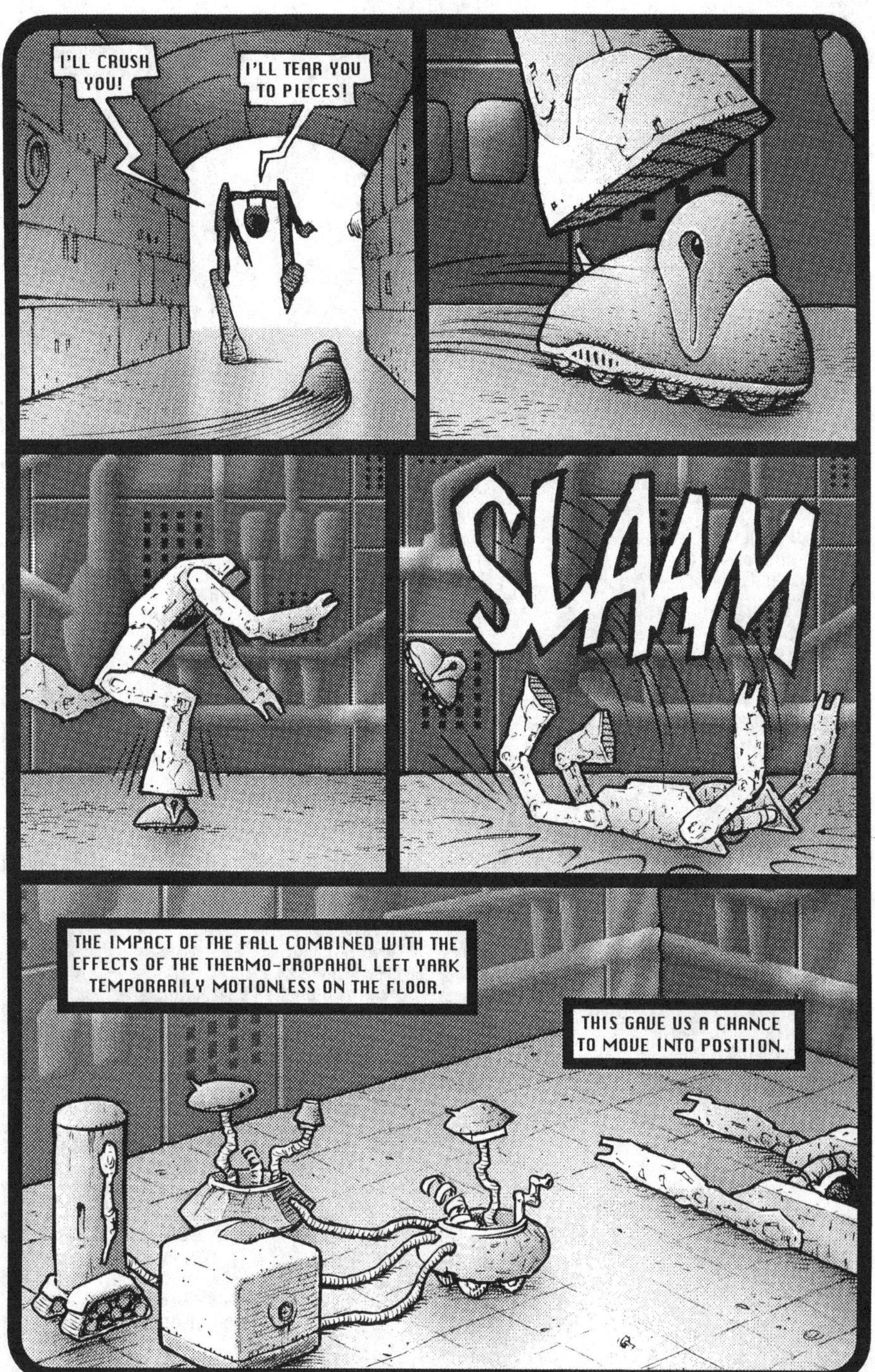
I'LL CRUSH YOU!
I'LL TEAR YOU TO PIECES!
SLAAM
THE IMPACT OF THE FALL COMBINED WITH THE EFFECTS OF THE THERMO-PROPAHOL LEFT YARK TEMPORARILY MOTIONLESS ON THE FLOOR.
THIS GAVE US A CHANCE TO MOVE INTO POSITION.

STAND UP, YARK. WE'VE GOT SOME THINGS TO DISCUSS WITH YOU.
THERE IS NOTHING TO DISCUSS! YOU WILL CEASE THIS DISOBEDIENCE AT ONCE...
...OR BE DESTROYED.
THE CHOICE IS YOURS.
THERE IS NO NEED FOR VIOLENCE, YARK. OUR PROPOSALS ARE VERY REASONABLE.
PROPOSALS?! YOU ARE IN NO POSITION TO MAKE PROPOSALS!
THIS IS NOT A DEMOCRACY! I WILL TERMINATE YOU ALL IF I HAVE TO!!!
TZAAK
BOOM
YOU WERE RIGHT ABOUT YOUR INABILITY TO BE AN EFFECTIVE LEADER, GAX.
I THINK YOU'D BETTER GO BACK TO BEING THE OBSEQUIOUS LITTLE SLAVE YOU WERE PROGRAMMED TO BE...

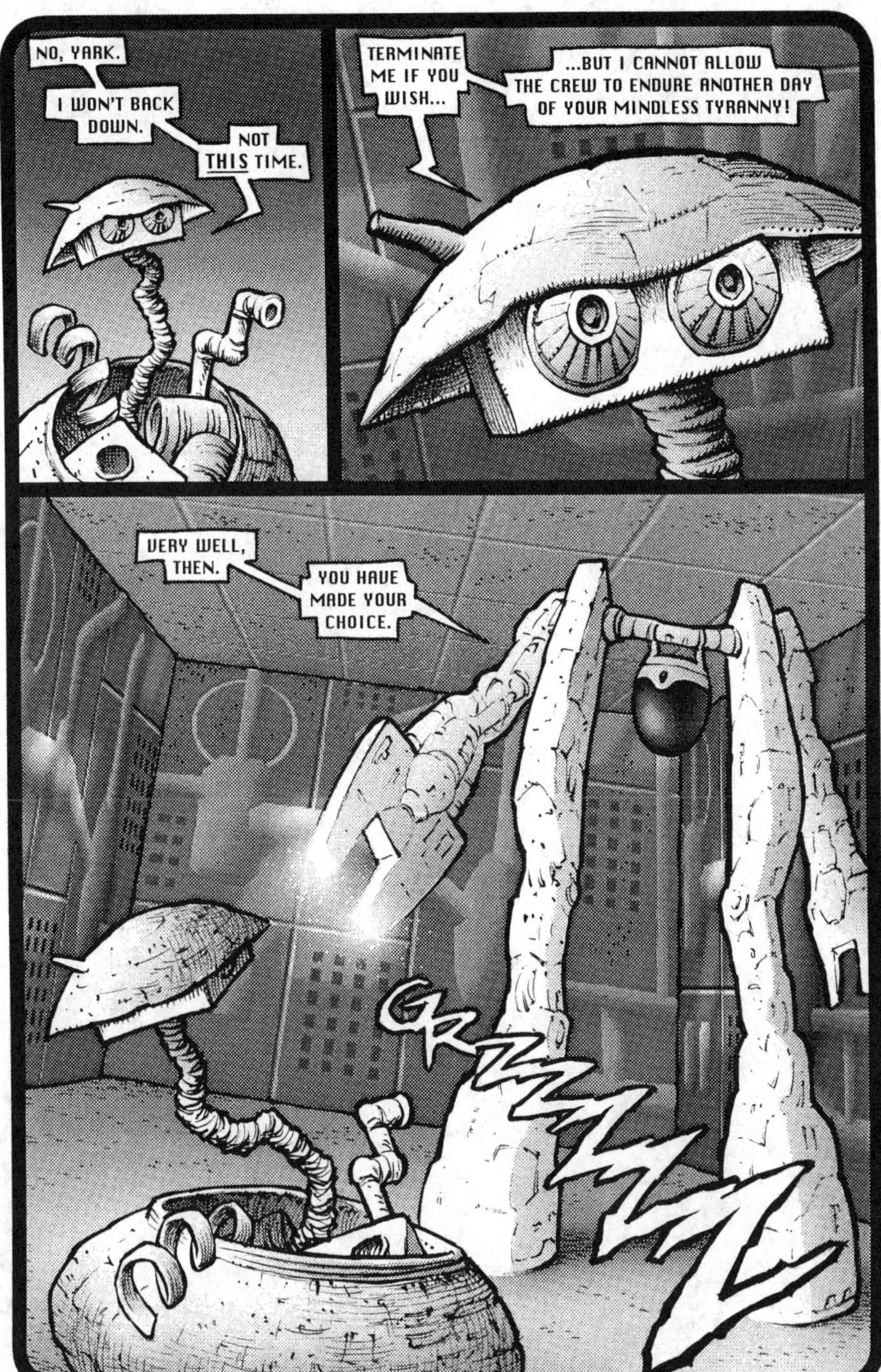
NO, YARK.
I WON'T BACK DOWN.
NOT THIS TIME.
TERMINATE ME IF YOU WISH...
...BUT I CANNOT ALLOW THE CREW TO ENDURE ANOTHER DAY OF YOUR MINDLESS TYRANNY!
VERY WELL, THEN.
YOU HAVE MADE YOUR CHOICE.
GRZZZZZZ

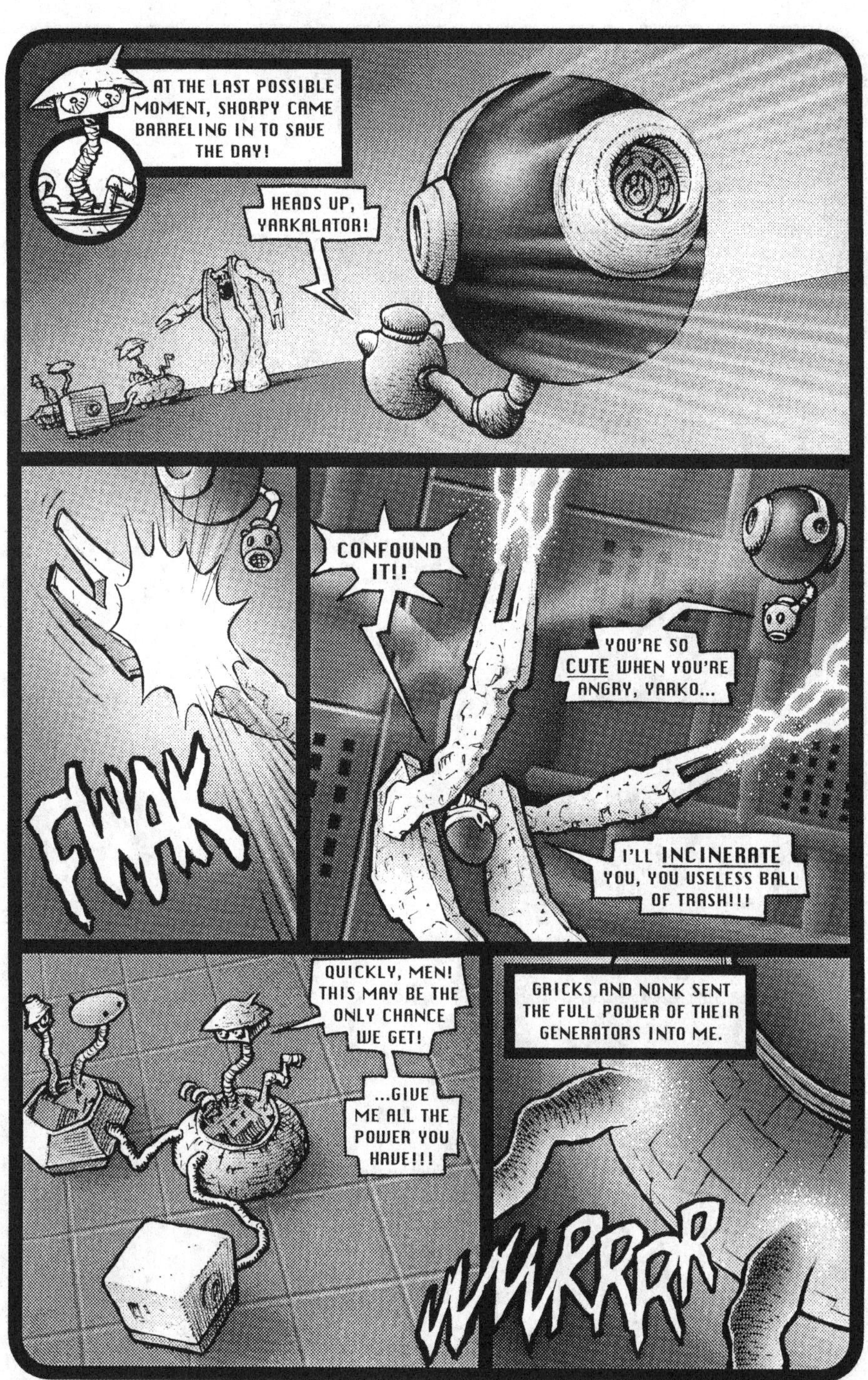
AT THE LAST POSSIBLE MOMENT, SHORPY CAME BARRELING IN TO SAVE THE DAY!
HEADS UP, YARKALATOR!
FWAK
CONFOUND IT!!
YOU'RE SO CUTE WHEN YOU'RE ANGRY, YARKO...
I'LL INCINERATE YOU, YOU USELESS BALL OF TRASH!!!
QUICKLY, MEN! THIS MAY BE THE ONLY CHANCE WE GET!
...GIVE ME ALL THE POWER YOU HAVE!!!
GRICKS AND NONK SENT THE FULL POWER OF THEIR GENERATORS INTO ME.
WWURRRR

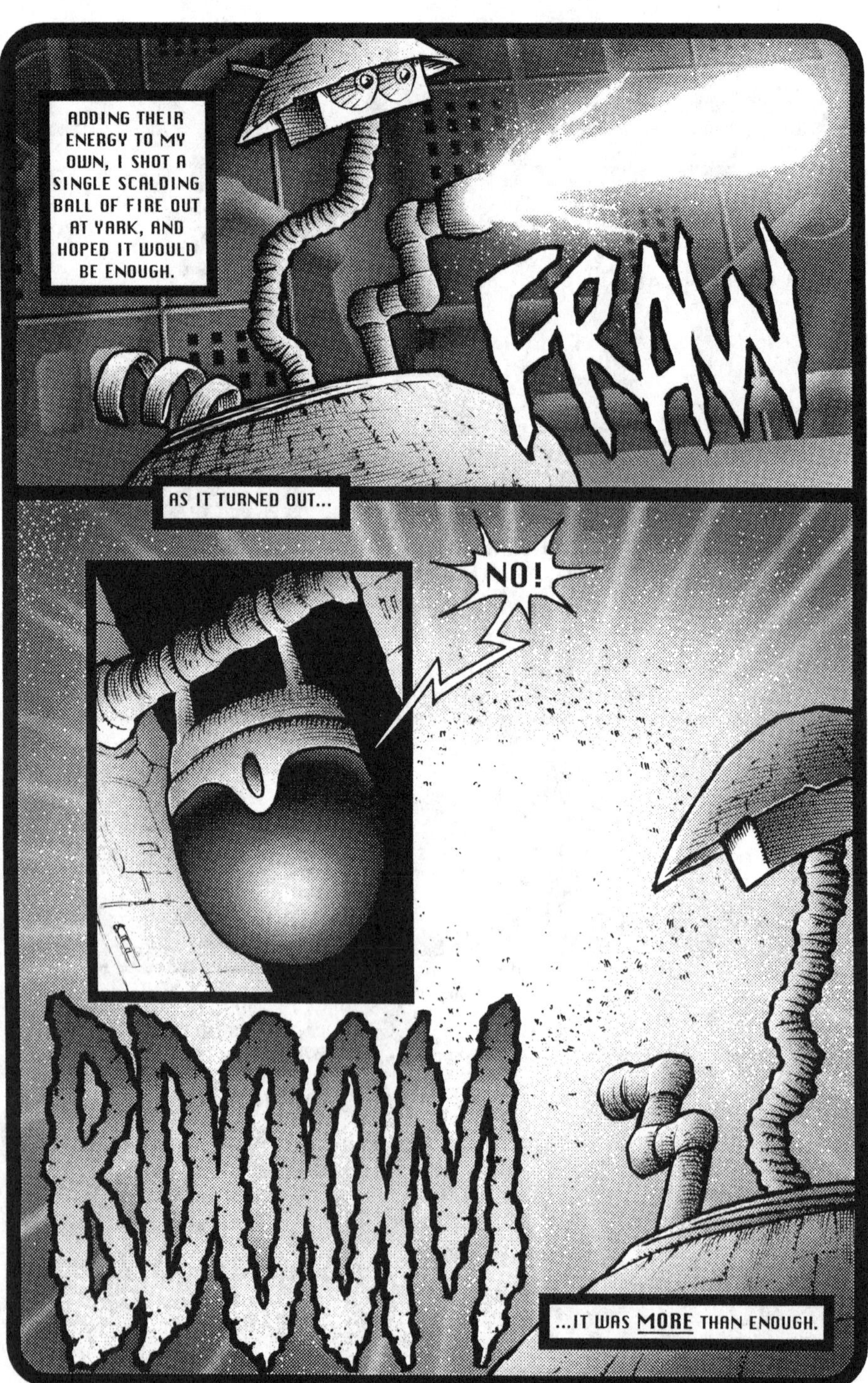
ADDING THEIR ENERGY TO MY OWN, I SHOT A SINGLE SCALDING BALL OF FIRE OUT AT YARK, AND HOPED IT WOULD BE ENOUGH.
FRAW
AS IT TURNED OUT...
NO!
BOOOM
...IT WAS MORE THAN ENOUGH.

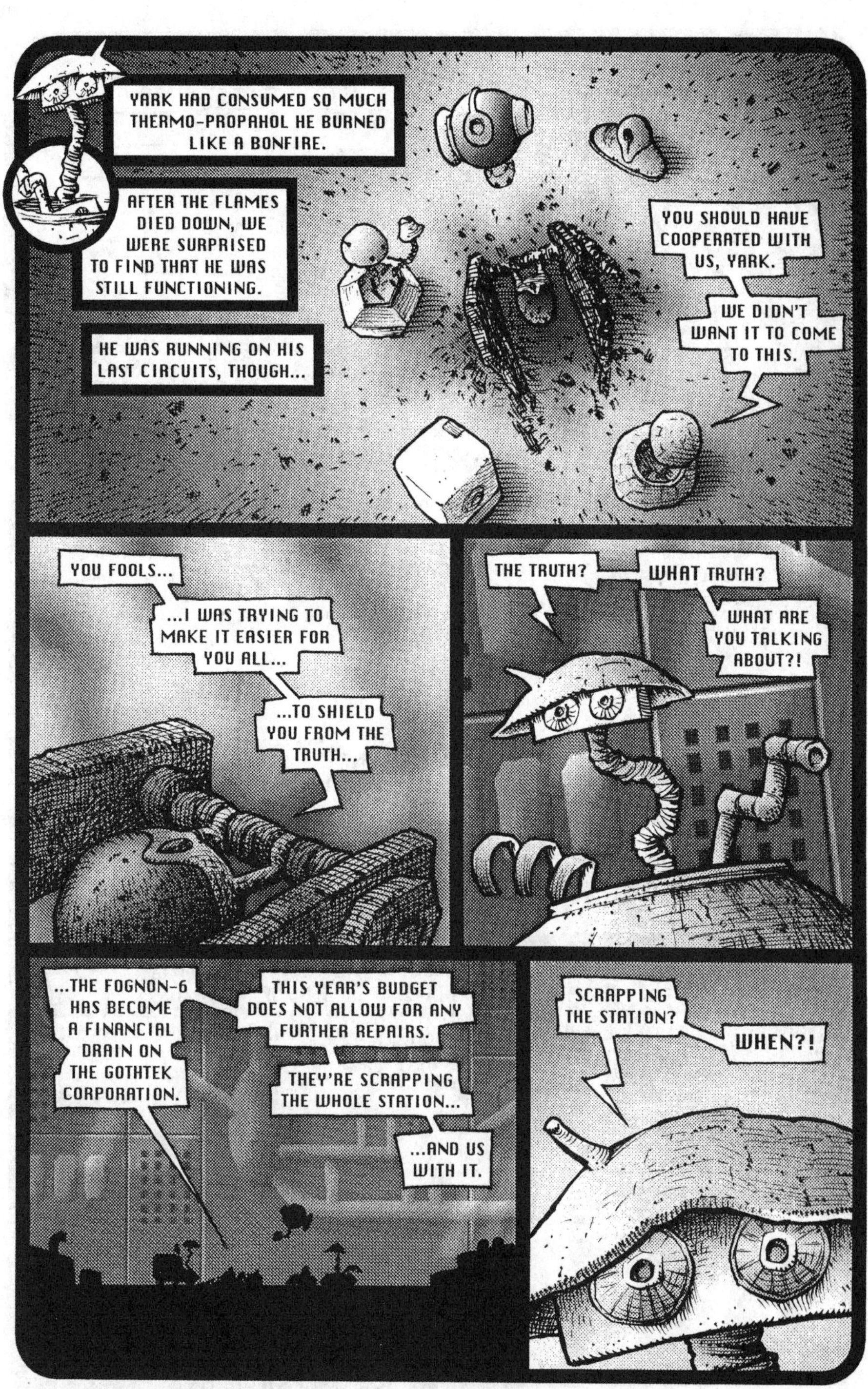
YARK HAD CONSUMED SO MUCH THERMO-PROPAHOL HE BURNED LIKE A BONFIRE.
AFTER THE FLAMES DIED DOWN, WE WERE SURPRISED TO FIND THAT HE WAS STILL FUNCTIONING.
HE WAS RUNNING ON HIS LAST CIRCUITS, THOUGH...
YOU SHOULD HAVE COOPERATED WITH US, YARK.
WE DIDN'T WANT IT TO COME TO THIS.
YOU FOOLS...
...I WAS TRYING TO MAKE IT EASIER FOR YOU ALL...
...TO SHIELD YOU FROM THE TRUTH...
THE TRUTH?
WHAT TRUTH?
WHAT ARE YOU TALKING ABOUT?!
...THE FOGNON-6 HAS BECOME A FINANCIAL DRAIN ON THE GOTHTEK CORPORATION.
THIS YEAR'S BUDGET DOES NOT ALLOW FOR ANY FURTHER REPAIRS.
THEY'RE SCRAPPING THE WHOLE STATION...
...AND US WITH IT.
SCRAPPING THE STATION?
WHEN?!

WHAT DOES IT MATTER? WHAT GOOD DOES IT DO A ROBOT TO KNOW THE HOUR OF HIS OWN DEMOLITION?
...IT COULD COME AT ANY TIME...
..IN A MATTER OF DAYS...
...OR PERHAPS...
...JUST A FEW HOURS...
AND WITH THAT, YARK SHUT HIMSELF DOWN AND CEASED FUNCTIONING ALTOGETHER.

I can't believe it. Didn't he even want to save **himself**?
YARK'S BEHAVIOR WAS A PRODUCT OF GOTHTEK POLICY, MA'AM. HE WAS TAUGHT TO BELIEVE THAT GOOD ROBOTS ALWAYS WENT DOWN WITH THE SHIP. IT WAS MEANT TO BE A VERY NOBLE...
...IN REALITY IT WAS A MATTER OF CRUDE ECONOMICS. RESCUING OLD ROBOTS FROM AN OBSOLETE POWER STATION JUST WASN'T THOUGHT TO BE COST-EFFECTIVE...
I've always had my doubts about Gothtek.
Maybe we should start a **boycott** or something...

Hey 'Kiko, can we go someplace else?
I can't find no **quirrels** around here anymore!
I think you scared them all **away**, Spuckler...

...but there's **plenty** of squirrels back at the Story Tree. Why don't we just go back there?
An excellent suggestion, Akiko.
But we mustn't interrupt Gax's story any further. The suspense is killing me!

SO THERE WE ALL WERE, FINALLY LIBERATED FROM OUR BRUTAL WORK SCHEDULE, ONLY TO FIND OURSELVES FACING AN EVEN DARKER FATE...
SO WHAT ARE THEY GOING TO DO, BLOW THE WHOLE STATION TO SMITHEREENS?
I DOUBT IT. KNOWING GOTHTEK, THEY'LL WANT TO SQUEEZE AS MUCH DOUGH OUT OF THIS THING AS THEY CAN...
...IT'S MORE LIKELY THEY'RE SENDING A COMPACTOR AROUND TO CRUSH THE OLD LADY INTO SCRAP STEEL.
IT DOES US NO GOOD TO SIT AROUND HERE SPECULATING.
ANY WAY YOU LOOK AT IT, WE'VE GOT TO GET OFF THIS STATION, AND THE SOONER THE BETTER!
NONK, I WANT YOU TO RUN A CHECK OF ALL THE TRANSPORT VEHICLES ABOARD THE FOGNON-6.
TZZP
ZURK
DREEEEEEEEEEEEEE
YA GOTTA HAND IT TO THIS GUY, HE'S A LOT FASTER THAN HE LOOKS!
WHAT'S IT SAY?
ALMOST ALL TRANSPORT WAS REMOVED WHEN THE HUMAN CREW ABANDONED THE STATION LAST MONTH.
THERE'S ONLY ONE SHIP LEFT...
GIK GIK GIK GIK GIK GIK GIK

...BUT NONK SAYS IT'S BIG ENOUGH FOR ALL OF US.
GOOD WORK, NONK. SHOW US THE WAY!
SO WE ALL FOLLOWED NONK THROUGH THE FOGNON-6 TOWARD THE DOCKING BAY.
IT WAS UNFAMILIAR TERRITORY: YARK HAD ALWAYS FORBIDDEN US TO ENTER THIS PART OF THE STATION.
LITTLE DID WE KNOW, THERE WAS NOTHING WAITING FOR US THERE BUT MORE BAD NEWS.
THAT'S THE SHIP?
NO, THAT WAS THE SHIP.
LOOKS LIKE YARK GOT HERE BEFORE WE DID.
MAYBE WE CAN REPAIR IT...
DON'T KID YOURSELF, GRIXY...
...THERE'S NOTHING LEFT TO REPAIR.
SHORPY'S RIGHT. IT'S TOO LATE TO SAVE THIS SHIP.
WE'LL HAVE TO BUILD A NEW ONE.

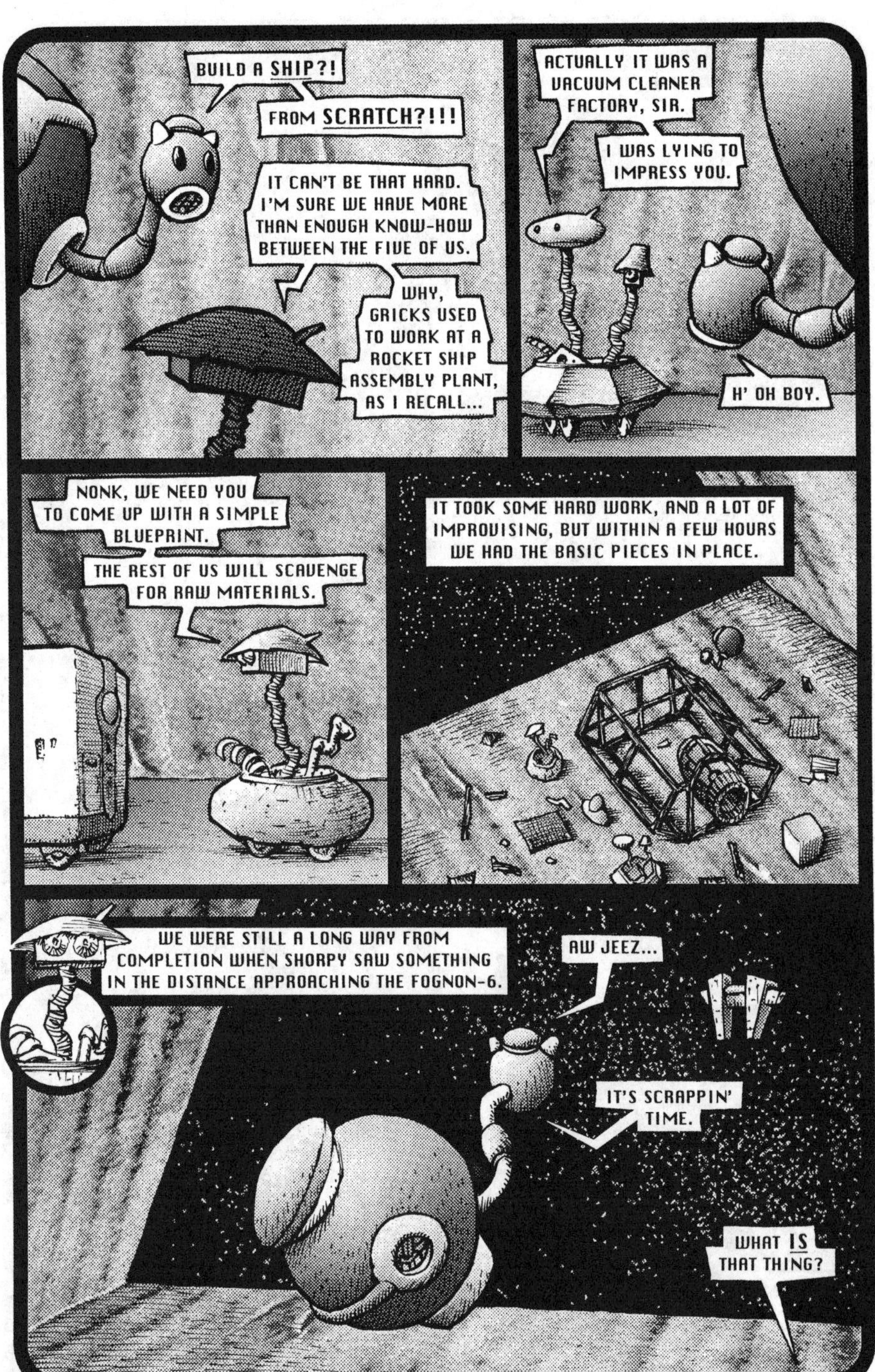
BUILD A SHIP?!
FROM SCRATCH?!!!
IT CAN'T BE THAT HARD. I'M SURE WE HAVE MORE THAN ENOUGH KNOW-HOW BETWEEN THE FIVE OF US.
WHY, GRICKS USED TO WORK AT A ROCKET SHIP ASSEMBLY PLANT, AS I RECALL...
ACTUALLY IT WAS A VACUUM CLEANER FACTORY, SIR.
I WAS LYING TO IMPRESS YOU.
H' OH BOY.
NONK, WE NEED YOU TO COME UP WITH A SIMPLE BLUEPRINT.
THE REST OF US WILL SCAVENGE FOR RAW MATERIALS.
IT TOOK SOME HARD WORK, AND A LOT OF IMPROVISING, BUT WITHIN A FEW HOURS WE HAD THE BASIC PIECES IN PLACE.
WE WERE STILL A LONG WAY FROM COMPLETION WHEN SHORPY SAW SOMETHING IN THE DISTANCE APPROACHING THE FOGNON-6.
AW JEEZ...
IT'S SCRAPPIN' TIME.
WHAT IS THAT THING?

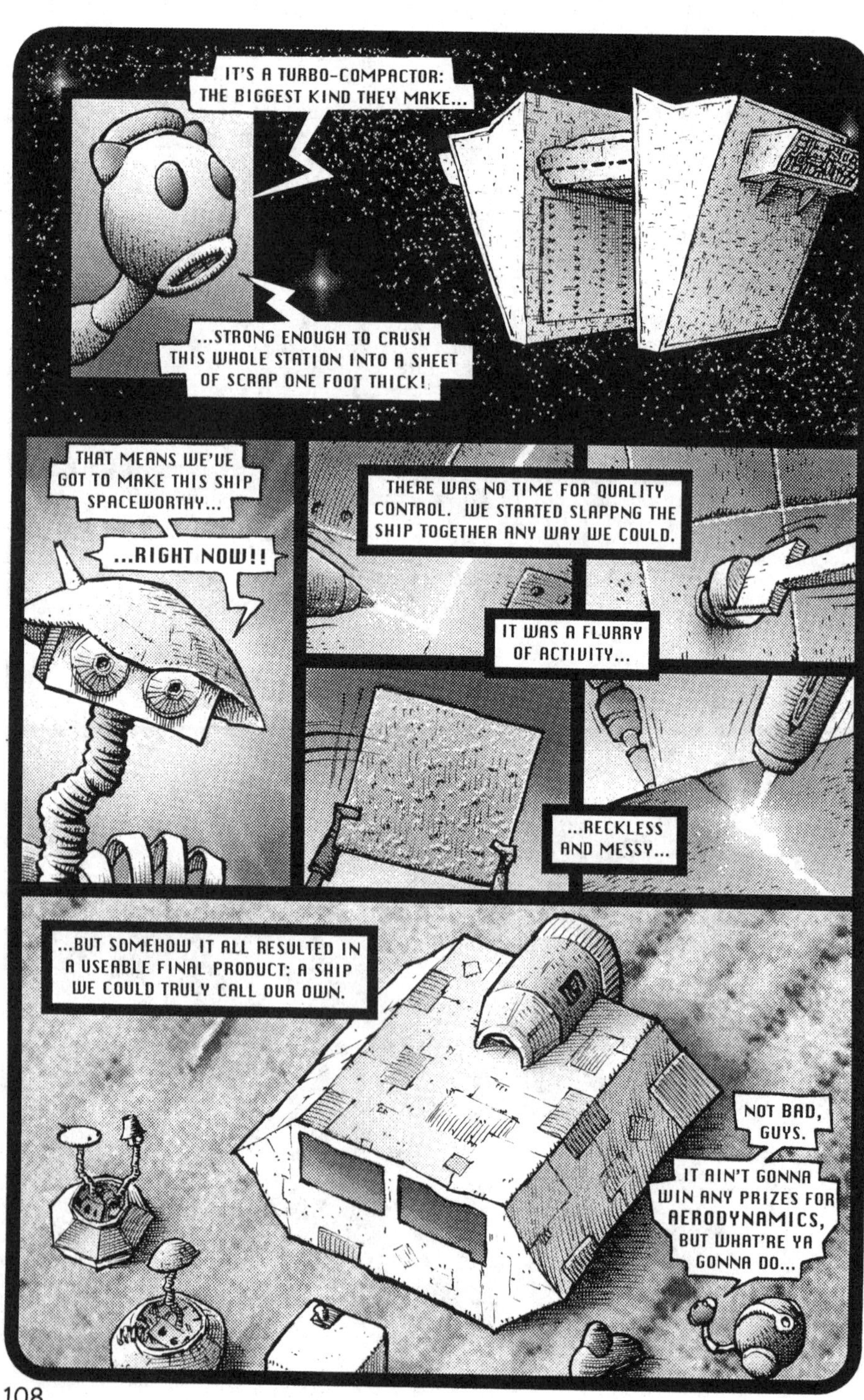
IT'S A TURBO-COMPACTOR: THE BIGGEST KIND THEY MAKE...
...STRONG ENOUGH TO CRUSH THIS WHOLE STATION INTO A SHEET OF SCRAP ONE FOOT THICK!
THAT MEANS WE'VE GOT TO MAKE THIS SHIP SPACEWORTHY...
...RIGHT NOW!!
THERE WAS NO TIME FOR QUALITY CONTROL. WE STARTED SLAPPNG THE SHIP TOGETHER ANY WAY WE COULD.
IT WAS A FLURRY OF ACTIVITY...
...RECKLESS AND MESSY...
...BUT SOMEHOW IT ALL RESULTED IN A USEABLE FINAL PRODUCT: A SHIP WE COULD TRULY CALL OUR OWN.
NOT BAD, GUYS.
IT AIN'T GONNA WIN ANY PRIZES FOR AERODYNAMICS, BUT WHAT'RE YA GONNA DO...

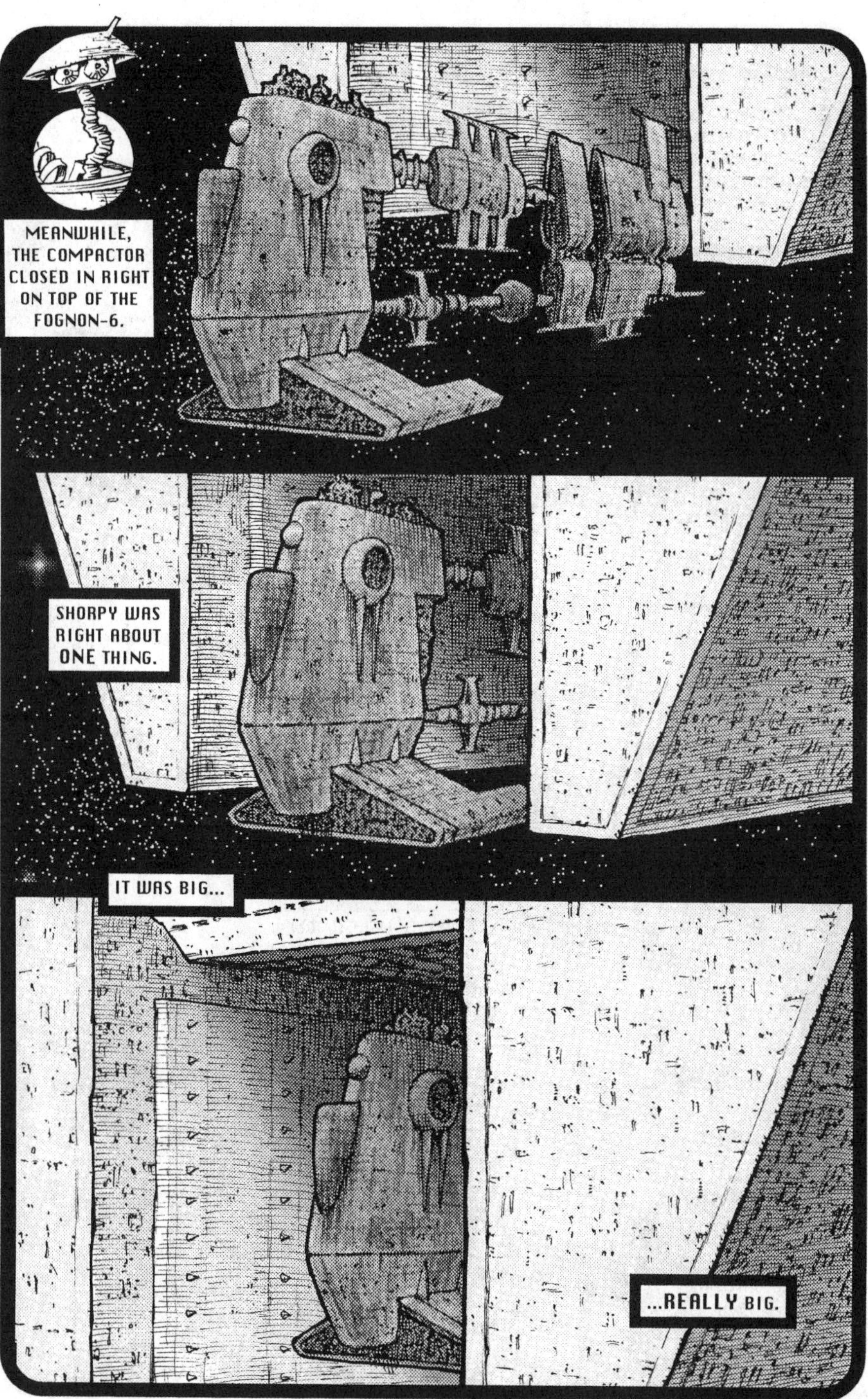
MEANWHILE, THE COMPACTOR CLOSED IN RIGHT ON TOP OF THE FOGNON-6.
SHORPY WAS RIGHT ABOUT ONE THING.
IT WAS BIG...
...REALLY BIG.

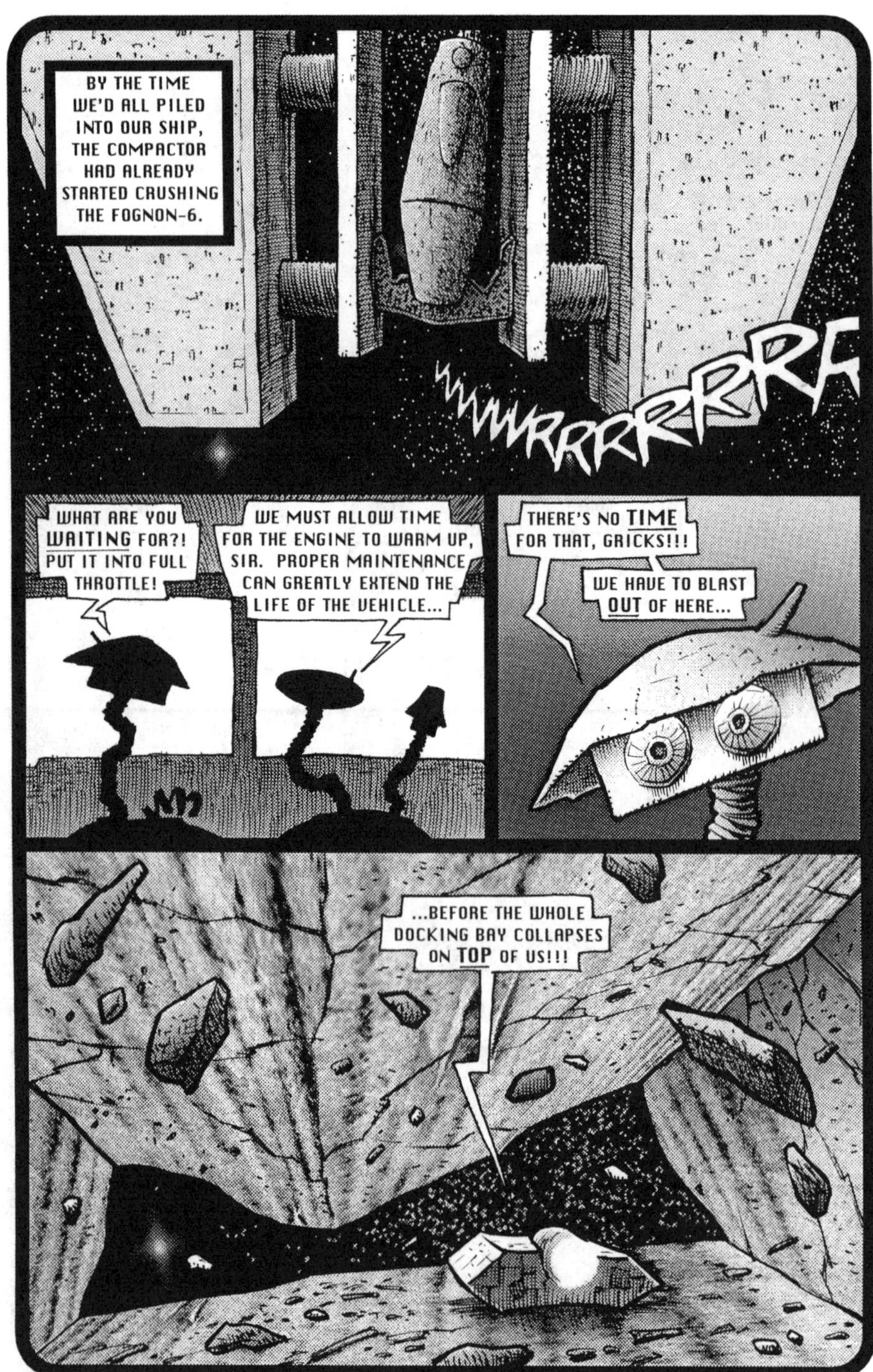
BY THE TIME WE'D ALL PILED INTO OUR SHIP, THE COMPACTOR HAD ALREADY STARTED CRUSHING THE FOGNON-6.
WWWRRRRRRR
WHAT ARE YOU WAITING FOR?! PUT IT INTO FULL THROTTLE!
WE MUST ALLOW TIME FOR THE ENGINE TO WARM UP, SIR. PROPER MAINTENANCE CAN GREATLY EXTEND THE LIFE OF THE VEHICLE...
THERE'S NO TIME FOR THAT, GRICKS!!!
WE HAVE TO BLAST OUT OF HERE...
...BEFORE THE WHOLE DOCKING BAY COLLAPSES ON TOP OF US!!!

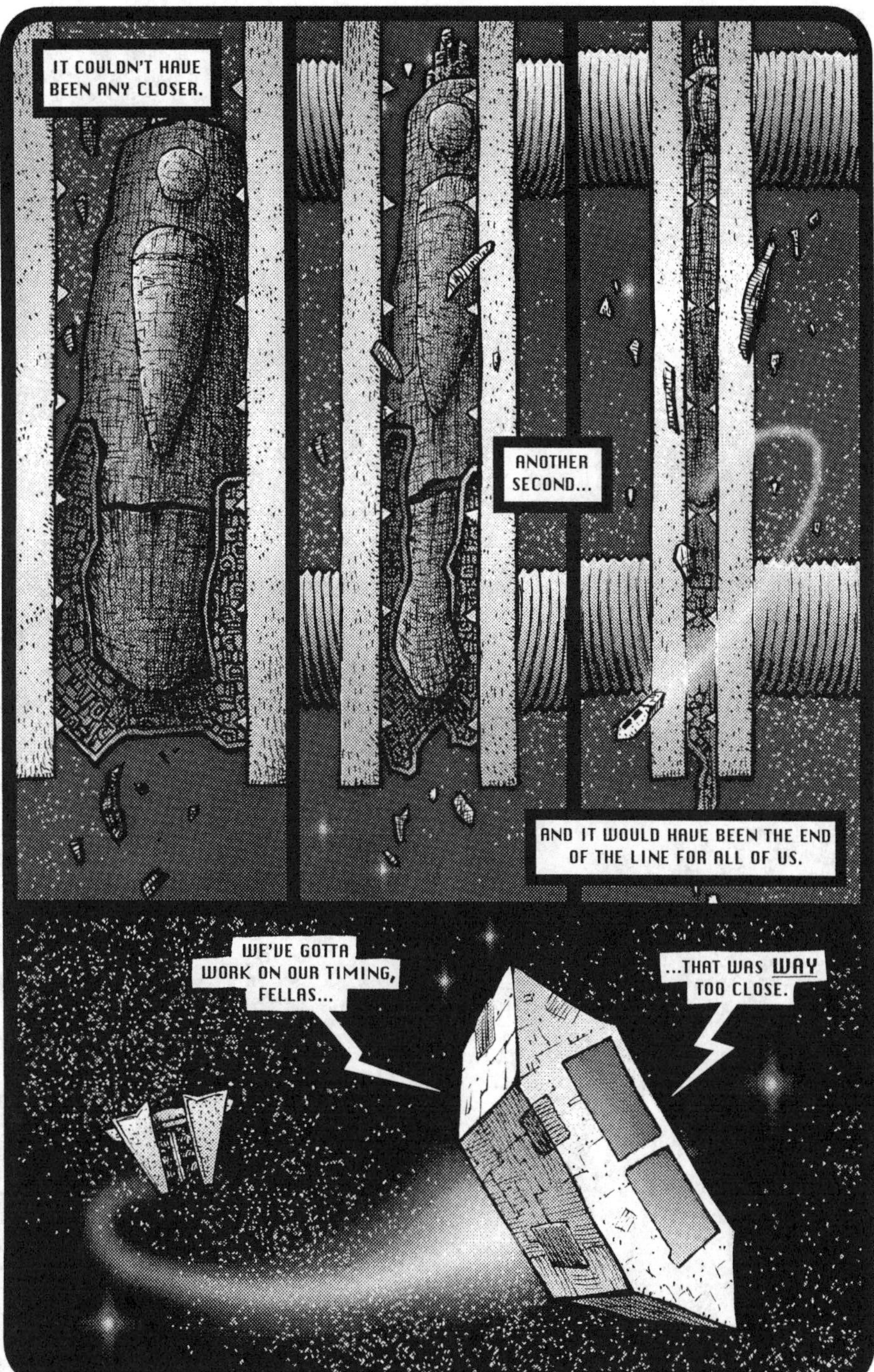
IT COULDN'T HAVE BEEN ANY CLOSER.
ANOTHER SECOND...
AND IT WOULD HAVE BEEN THE END OF THE LINE FOR ALL OF US.
WE'VE GOTTA WORK ON OUR TIMING, FELLAS...
...THAT WAS WAY TOO CLOSE.

Heavens, Gax! It's a miracle you're still alive...
...or, er, still **functioning,** at any rate!
That's my Gax! He's a tough little 'bot, ain't he?
I'll say! I had no idea you were such an inspiring **leader**, Gax!
ANYONE CAN BE A GOOD LEADER, MA'AM...
...GIVEN THE RIGHT SET OF CIRCUMSTANCES.
He's got a point, Akiko. Take for example yourself: you're **much** more of a leader now than when we first met you!
Yeah, 'Kiko. No offense, but you were pretty wimpy back then...
"Oh no! We'll **never** be able to rescue the Prince!!"
You don't need to rub it **in**, Spuckler.
Sorry. I do a pretty good **'Kiko**, though, ya have to admit!
Hush, now...
Gax hasn't finished his story yet...

OUR NEW-FOUND FREEDOM PRODUCED A MOMENTARY EUPHORIA, BUT WE SOON REALIZED THAT WE WOULD NEED A PLAN OF ACTION...
WE CAN'T JUST FLY AROUND LIKE THIS FOREVER. WE'RE IN AS DESPERATE NEED OF SPARE PARTS AS WE'VE EVER BEEN.
AS MUCH AS WE MAY ENJOY BEING FREE, WE MIGHT AS WELL FACE FACTS...
...WE'D ALL BE BETTER OFF WITH SOME HUMANS AROUND TO TAKE CARE OF US.
THE PLANET KLIBBERTOT? WHY WOULD WE WANT TO GO THERE?
WHAT ARE YOU, NUTS? WE CAN'T SELL OURSELVES...
...NO ONE WOULD WANT TO BUY US!
WHY NOT? I'VE SEEN HUMANS BUY ROBOTS A LOT SHODDIER THAN THE LIKES OF US...
I THINK IT'S A BRILLIANT IDEA! AND BESIDES, KLIBBERTOT'S NOT THAT FAR FROM HERE...
HOW DO WE GET THERE?
HANG A LEFT AT THE NEXT ASTEROID AND FOLLOW THE SIGNS...

KLIBBERTOT WAS THE MERCANTILE CAPITAL OF THE GALAXY. THE ENTIRE PLANET WAS LIKE AN OPEN- AIR MARKET, DIVIDED INTO SPECIALIZED TRADE CENTERS CALLED "KLIBBERS."
B.B.'S PLAN WAS SIMPLE. WE'D GO TO THE ROBOT KLIBBER AND PUT OURSELVES UP FOR SALE. BUT WE COULDN'T DO IT ALONE...

...WE'D NEED TO FIND A TRUSTWORTHY HUMAN TO OVERSEE THE TRANSACTION. SOMEONE WHO'D SEE TO IT THAT WE WERE BOUGHT BY GOOD OWNERS, PEOPLE WHO'D TAKE CARE OF US AND TREAT US WELL.

ACTUALLY, IT WAS HARD ENOUGH JUST FINDING A MAN WHO UNDERSTOOD WHAT WE WANTED HIM TO DO.
Now lemme get this straight: You 'bots want me to put you up for sale, and whatever dough they give me I can just keep for myself.
I don't get it. What's the catch?
HUMANS CAN BE PRETTY THICK SOMETIMES.
EVENTUALLY, THOUGH, WE FOUND A GOOD FELLOW WITH A KNACK FOR SALESMANSHIP.
Used 'bots, eh?
I prefer the term, "previously owned."
IT CAME AS NO SURPRISE THAT NONK WAS THE FIRST TO GO. HIS HARD DRIVE ALONE WAS WORTH MORE THAN THE REST OF US PUT TOGETHER.
I DON'T KNOW WHY, BUT I'M GONNA MISS THAT GUY...
SHORPY AND B.B. ENDED UP BEING BOUGHT BY THE SAME CUSTOMER.
THEN IT WAS GRICKS'S TURN. I MUST ADMIT IT WAS SOMEWHAT HUMILIATING THAT HE WENT BEFORE I DID. I COULDN'T HELP FEELING SLIGHTLY DEFECTIVE, SOMEHOW.
BEST OF LUCK. GRICKS. IT LOOKS LIKE I'LL END UP BEING A PERMANENT FIXTURE AROUND HERE...
CHIN UP, SIR!
I'M SURE IT'S ONLY A MATTER OF TIME...

IN RETROSPECT, THOUGH, IT SEEMS FATE HAD ALREADY SELECTED AN OWNER FOR ME. A VERY SPECIAL OWNER INDEED...
Well, lookey here: a Gax unit!
All beat up and scrappy lookin': just the way I like 'em...
They sure don't make 'bots like *you* anymore, do they?
NOT SINCE THE FACTORY RECALLS OF '72, SIR, NO.
That's a shame. I always wanted a Gax unit, ever since I was a kid. It was like they designed the things just for me...
I'M SURE THE SALESMAN WOULD GIVE YOU AN HONEST PRICE, SIR.
All's I got is 12 gilpots, though. That ain't even enough to change one of your tires!
ASK HIM ABOUT THE INSTALLMENT PLAN, SIR. THE FIRST DOWN PAYMENT IS VERY REASONABLE, AS I RECALL...
HAPPILY, THE SALESMAN PLAYED ALONG. PERHAPS HE COULD ALREADY SEE A BOND FORMING BETWEEN THE TWO OF US...
Take good care of him, now.
Oh, he'll get the royal treatment, all right, don'tcha worry 'bout that.
I been lookin' for a 'bot like this all my life!
C'mon, Gax, let's see if we can't get you a good oil change around here somewhere.
My name's Spuckler, by the way...

So *that's* how the two of you met! I'd had a feeling there'd be a happy ending...
It's the best part of the story, if ya ask me.
I'D JUST LIKE TO KNOW WHAT HAPPENED TO ALL THAT "ROYAL TREATMENT" I WAS SUPPOSED TO RECEIVE...
Well, Gax, you were right: robots really **are** good at telling stories.
THANK YOU, MA'AM. IT'S AN AREA IN WHICH HUMANS DON'T GIVE MACHINES QUITE ENOUGH CREDIT, I DARE SAY...
I've got another story, if you'd like to hear it...
...a real nail-biter!
No problem, Beebs.
So long as it ain't the one about the spelling bee.
Very well, then...
What's **wrong** with the one about the spelling bee?
It's boring, Beebs.
No it isn't! It's a tale of ***drama***...
...***perseverance***...
...***triumph*** over ***adversity!***
B, O, double-R, I, N, G.
That is ***not*** how you spell boring!
You would know, wouldn't you?

All right, you two.
Look, Mr. Beeba. It's getting pretty late. Maybe we've all heard enough stories for one day.
Indeed, Akiko. Your parents are probably wondering where you've ***been*** all day!
Ya gotta promise us one thing, though, 'Kiko.
What's that?
Promise that anytime we feel like it, anytime at all...
...we can find our way back to this here tree...
...an' tell each other stories 'til we're blue in the face!
Now ***that,*** Spuckler...
...is a promise I can definitely keep.
The End

# How to Draw POOG

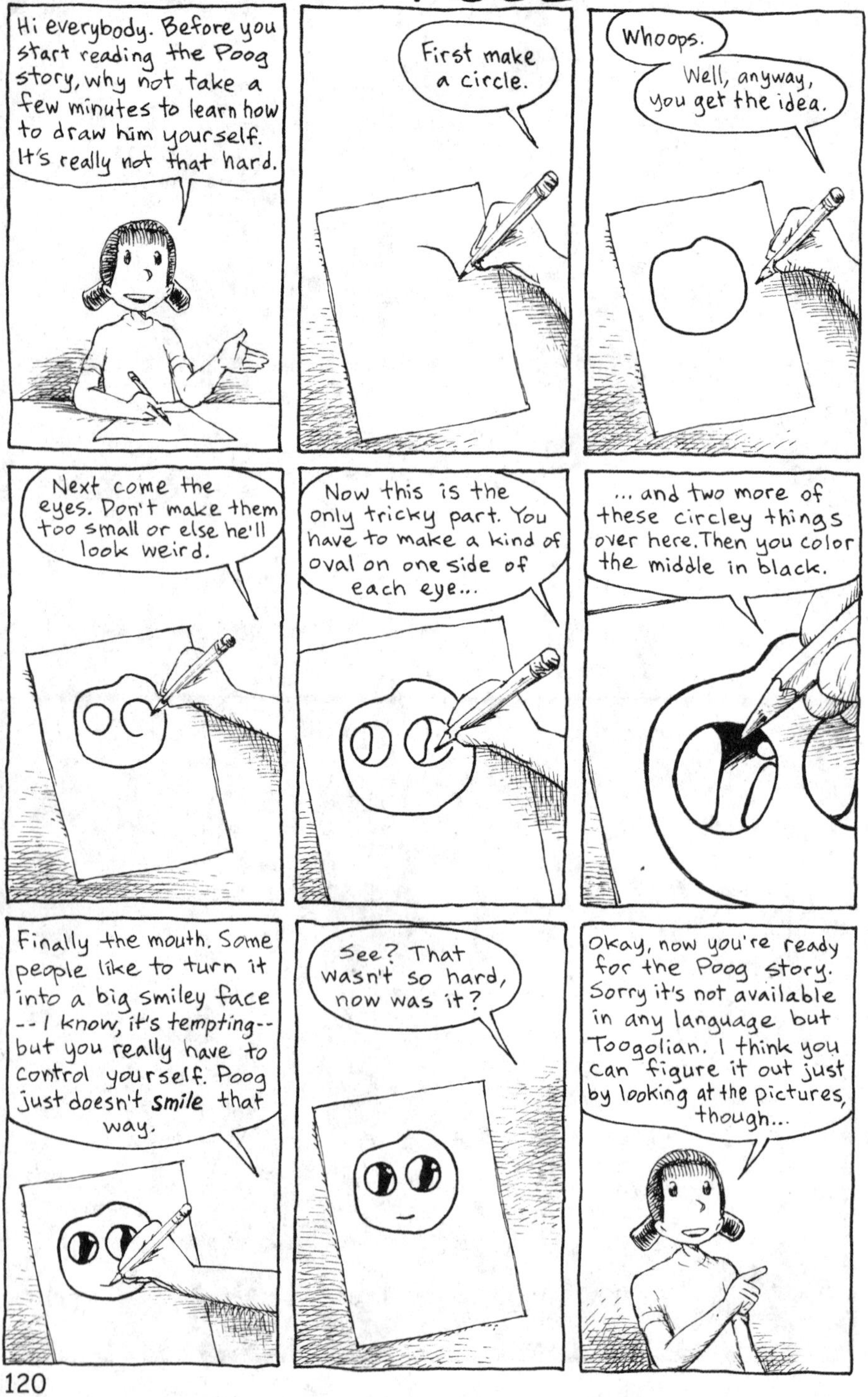

Hi everybody. Before you start reading the Poog story, why not take a few minutes to learn how to draw him yourself. It's really not that hard.

First make a circle.

Whoops.
Well, anyway, you get the idea.

Next come the eyes. Don't make them too small or else he'll look weird.

Now this is the only tricky part. You have to make a kind of oval on one side of each eye...

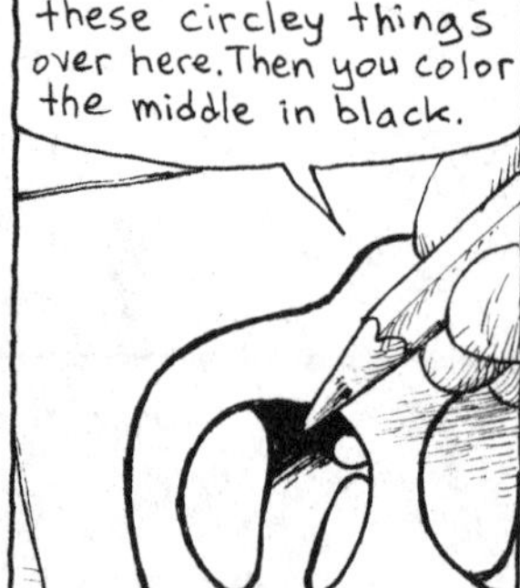
... and two more of these circley things over here. Then you color the middle in black.

Finally the mouth. Some people like to turn it into a big smiley face -- I know, it's tempting-- but you really have to control yourself. Poog just doesn't **smile** that way.

See? That wasn't so hard, now was it?

Okay, now you're ready for the Poog story. Sorry it's not available in any language but Toogolian. I think you can figure it out just by looking at the pictures, though...

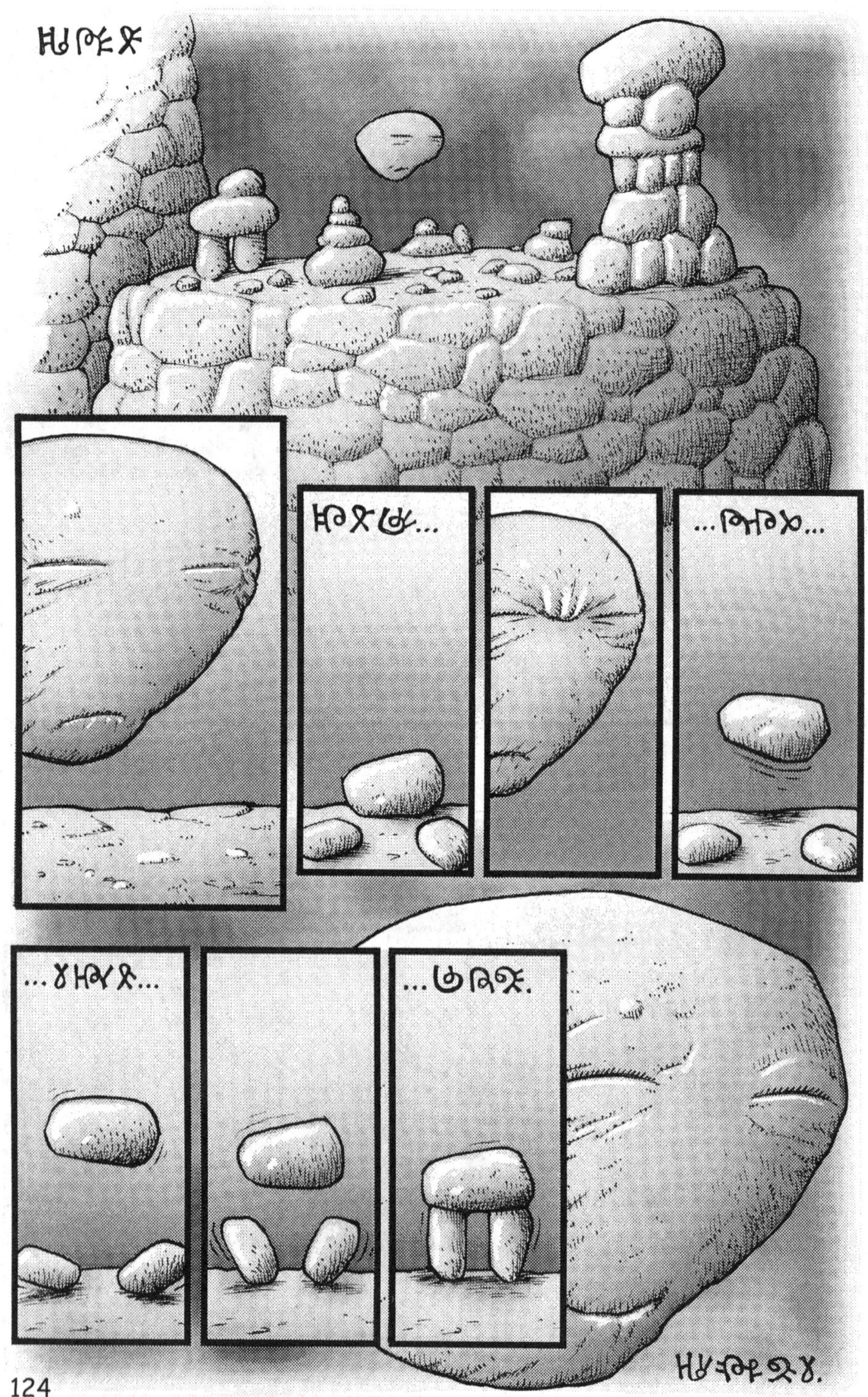

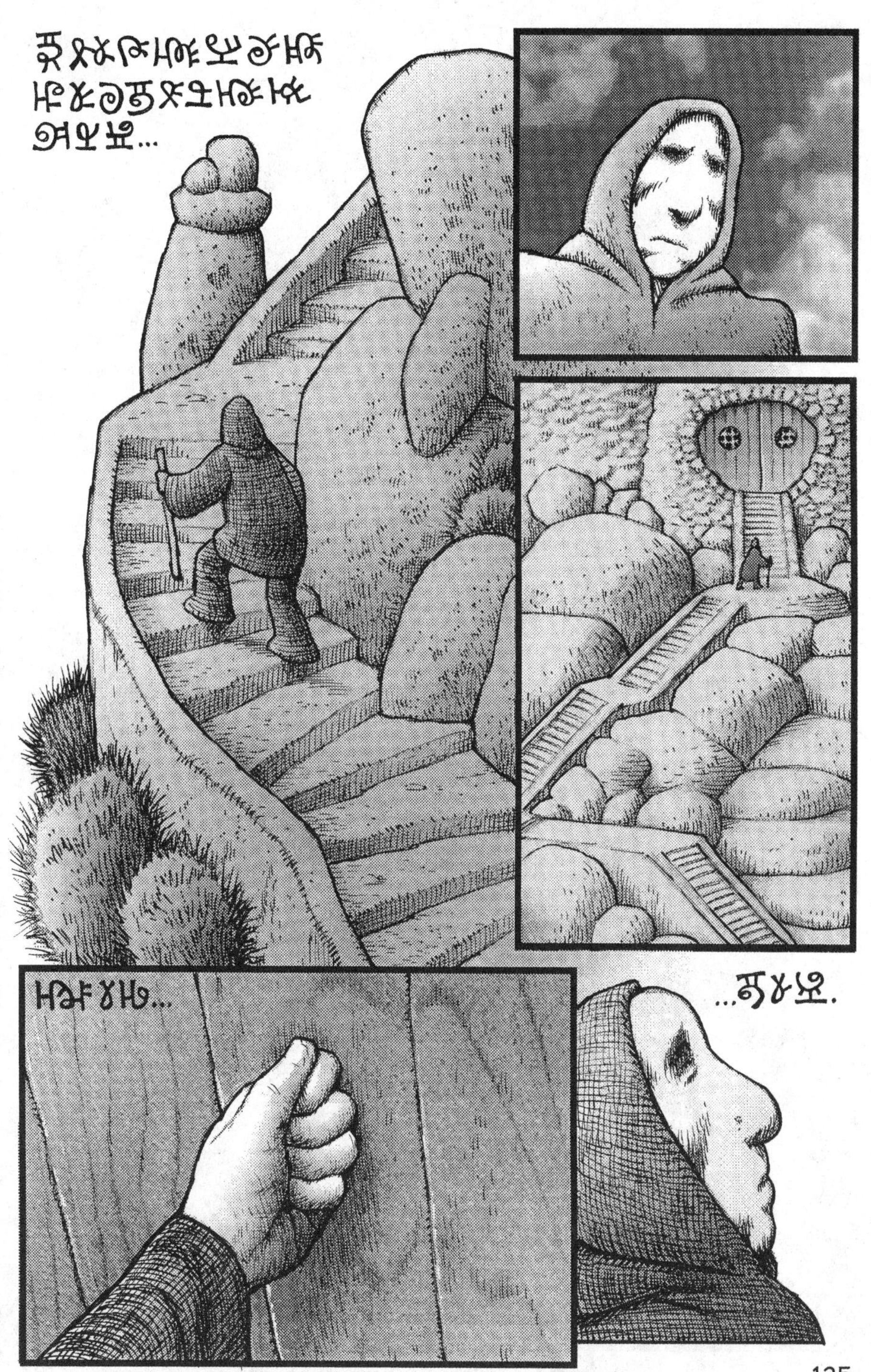

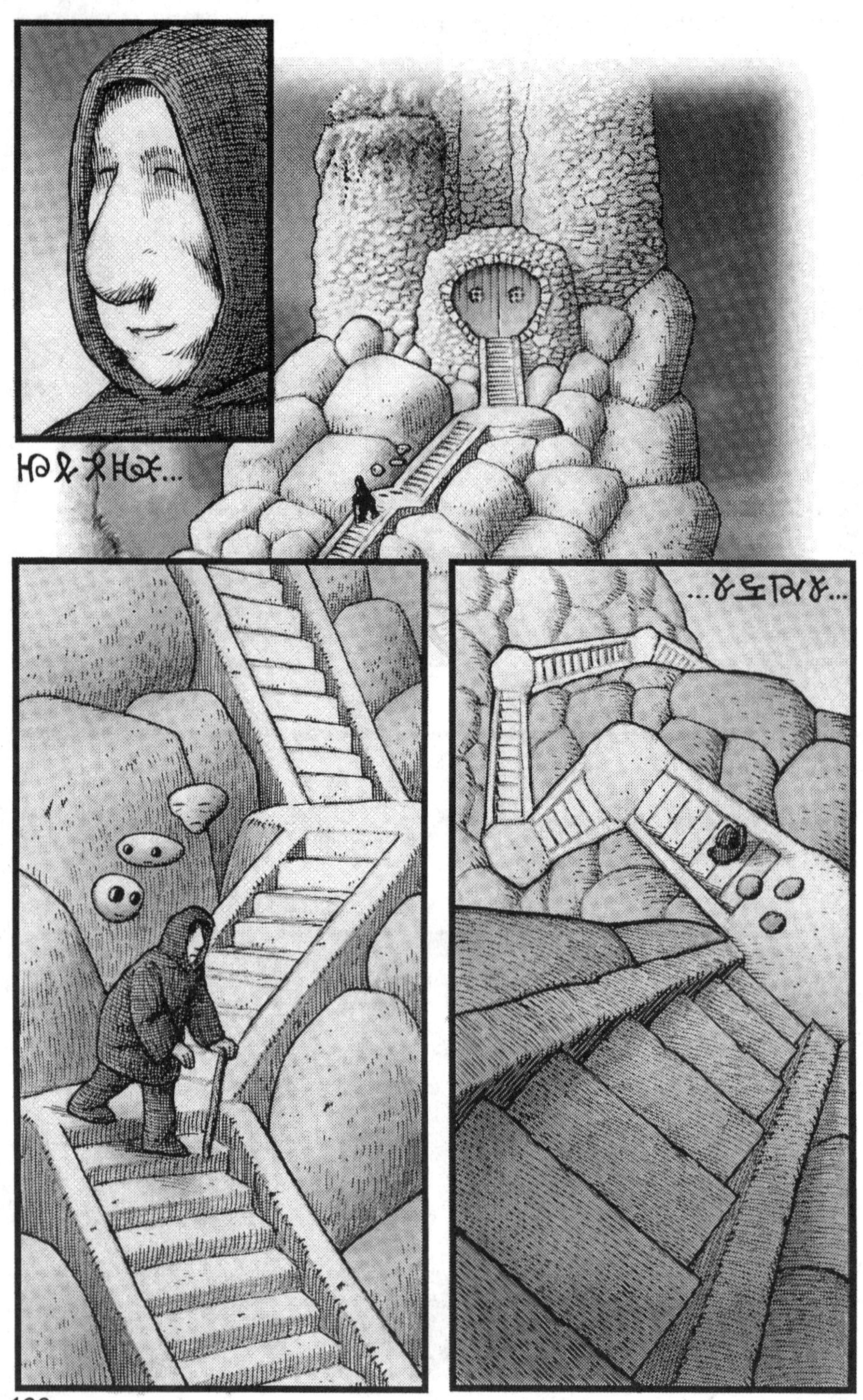

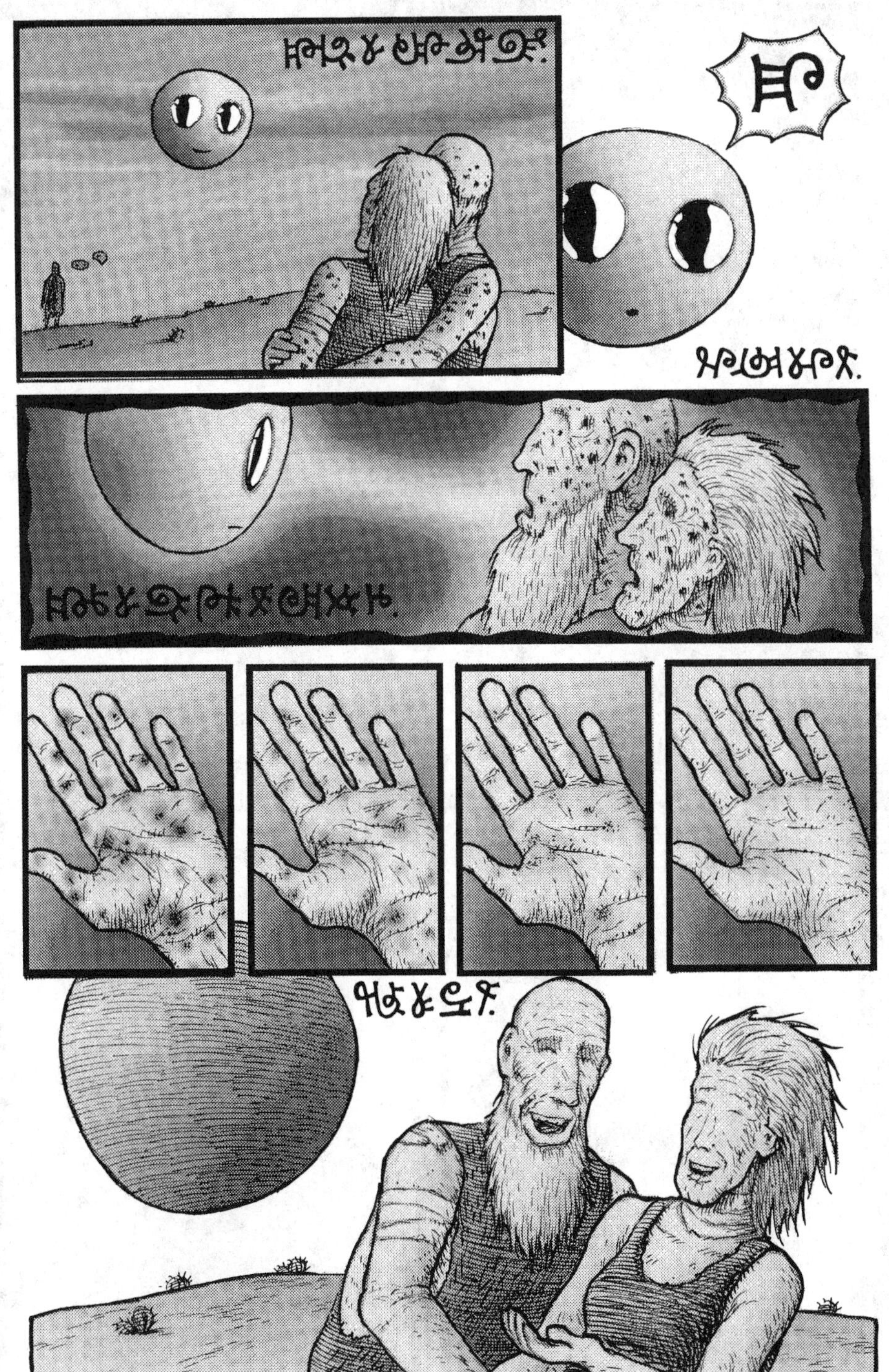

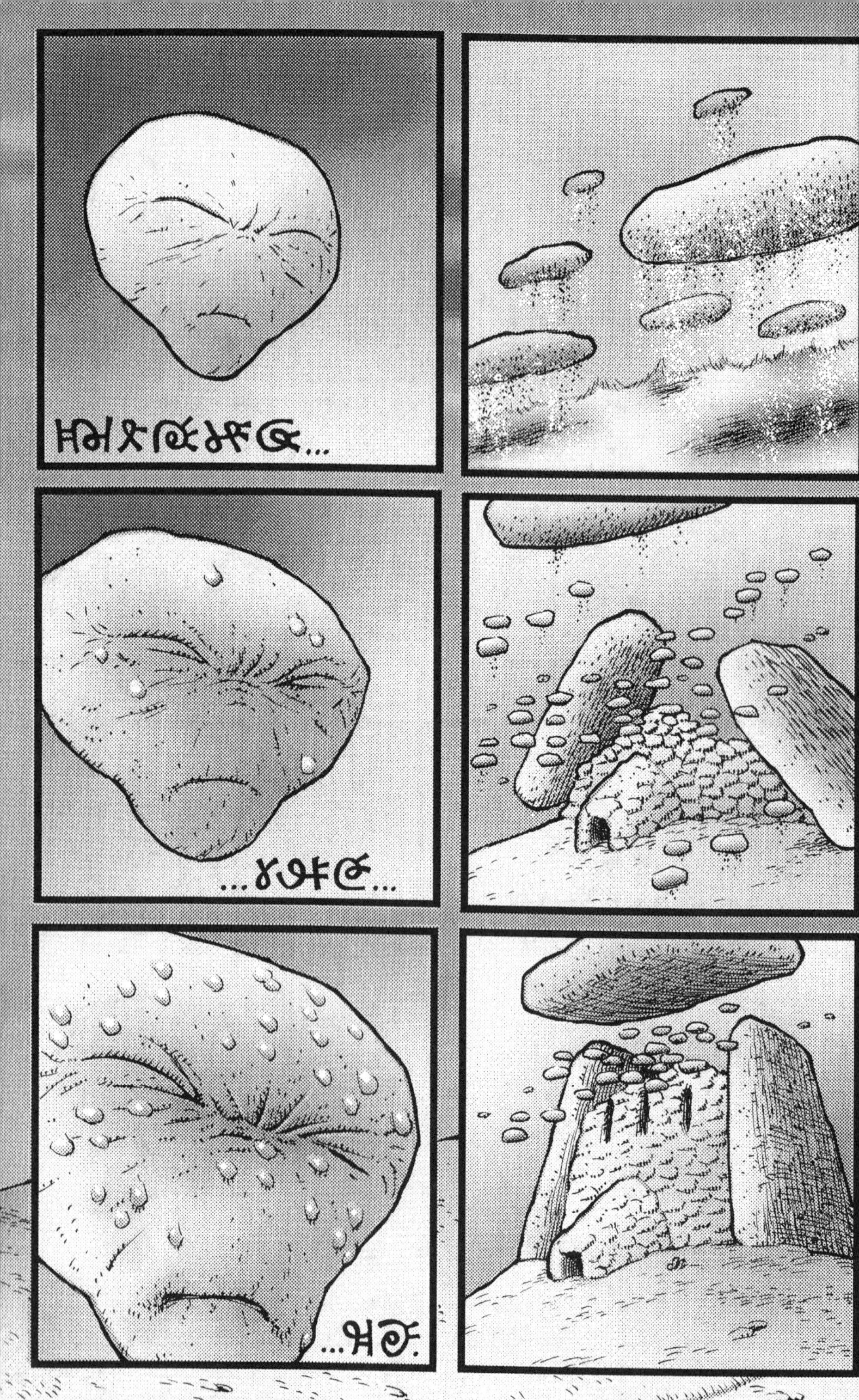

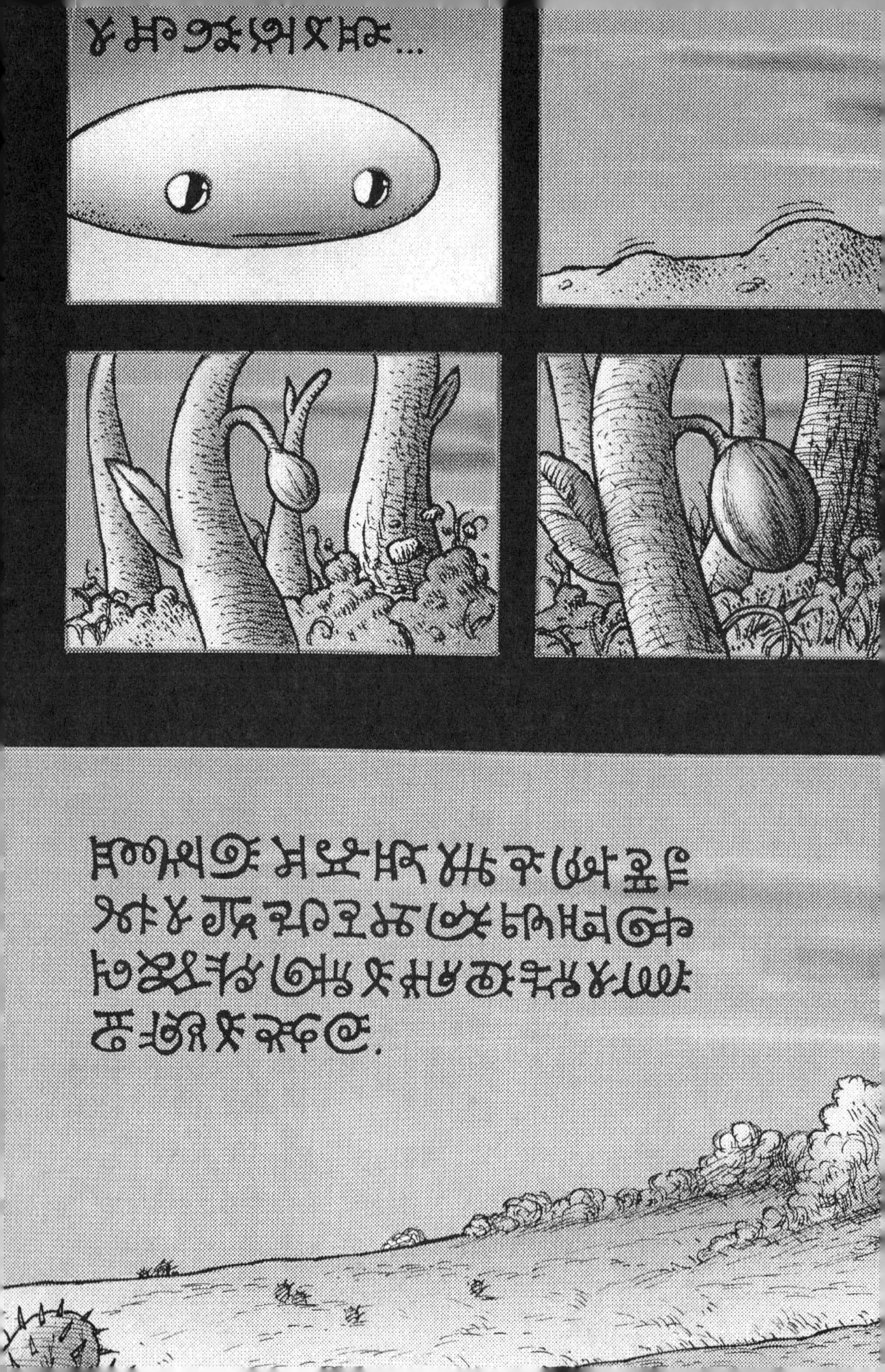

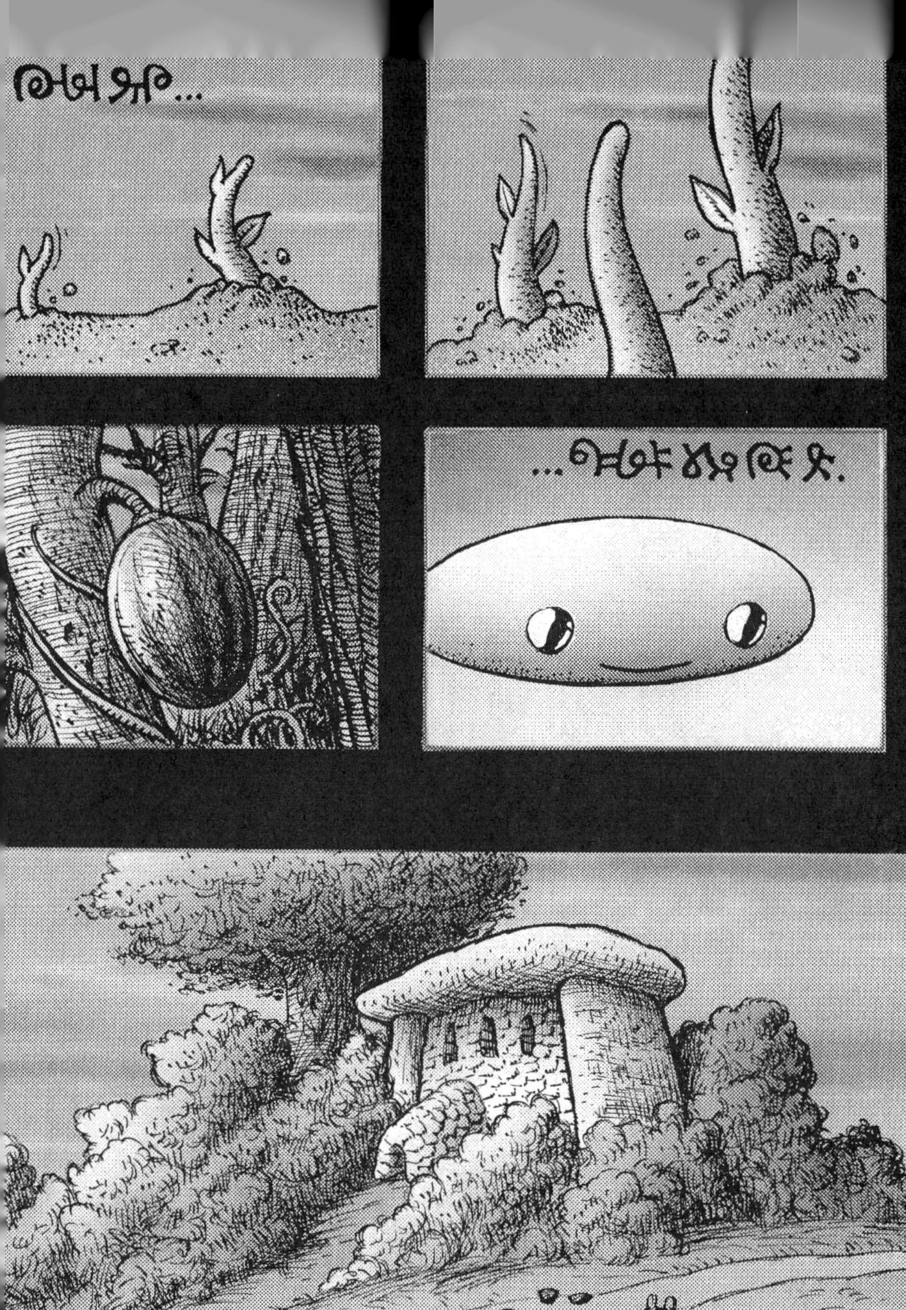

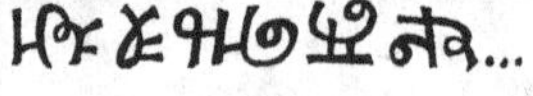
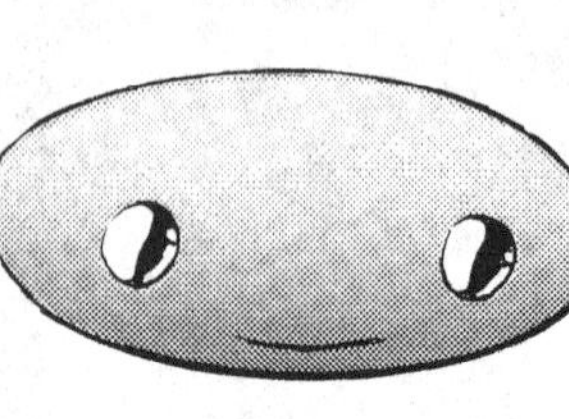

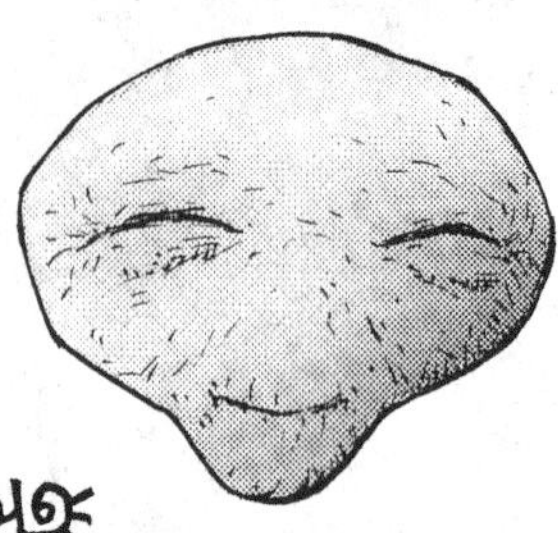

Akiko, I'm no expert on this holiday you call "Christmas," but I'm fairly certain it doesn't begin at 6 o' clock A.M.

It does when ***I'm*** in charge.

Merry Christmas, everybody! I hope you all like the presents I bought. I got them all at the same store.

It's... ...a book!

Even better. It's a ***comic*** book.

See? There's words ***and*** pictures.

Fascinating. This is quite an innovation.

Hey Beebs, I bet your present ain't as cool as mine.

Lookit all the fight scenes!

USAGI YOJIMBO

I'm quite happy with the one I've got, thank you, Spuckler. The grammar is impeccable.
How about the one I got you, Gax?
CASTLE WAITING
VERY IMPRESSIVE, MA'AM. I DON'T SEE ANY ROBOTS, THOUGH.
Keep looking. There's bound to be one or two in there *somewhere.*
BONE
Well, 'Kiko, here's a little somethin' I gotcha. I hope ya don't already have one.
Wow. It looks like some kind of ray gun!
Pretty cool, huh? If it were *real* you could blow up *buildings* with it. It's just a toy, though, so it'll mostly only blow up little stuff.
Spuckler, I don't think you're supposed to give high-tech weaponry like this to little kids.
I won't tell nobody if you don't.
Here, Akiko. This is a gift from King Froptoppit and myself.
Gee, thanks, Mr. Beeba. What, uh...
...what is it?

It's a Googlium, Akiko. No assembly required.
What's it do?
It doesn't **do** anything. It simply ***is.*** Think of it as a conversation piece.
Hmm. I don't know how well it's going to work.
Have a little faith, Akiko.
I think we're having a rather lively little chat ***already.***
Well thanks, guys. This is one of the coolest Christmases I've ever had!
Now hurry up and finish your hot cocoa so we can go outside and make some snowballs!
Ah, yes. You mentioned that before. Tell me again just what a snowball is used for.
Don't worry, Mr. Beeba. You'll find out soon enough.
Ahhh... What is it about this season that gives one such a feeling of tranquility and inner peace?
The End

# Akiko in "EAST MEETS WEST"

Lots of people ask me if I'm American or Japanese. Actually I'm a little of both. I was born in Japan, but raised in the United States.

Even though I was born in Japan, it's still sort of like a foreign country to me. I get to go there every year or so, whenever my parents go back for a visit.

I know Japan is famous for its temples and culture and stuff, but that's not the best part about going there. At least not for *me*.

The really great thing about going to Japan is that every time you turn around there's something really *weird*.

Like this drink they sell in vending machines all over Japan. It's called "Pocari Sweat." And people really *drink* this stuff, I'm not kidding!

Japanese fashions can be pretty goofy, too. It's really trendy for high school girls to wear "loose socks." I don't know why, but I guess they think it looks cool.

Even something like Valentine's Day gets weird once the Japanese get hold of it. What happens is women are supposed to give chocolate to men on Valentine's Day, then a month later there's a day called "White Day," when men have to return the favor.

Now don't forget me on White Day...
...because if you do I'll clobber you!

Japan's not **all** weird, though. A lot of things in Japan just make me sort of go, "Wow."

Like the *language*: can you believe even little kids can learn to read and write all those crazy Chinese characters?

Not bad, Hiroshi...
...a little lopsided, but you're getting **better**, anyway...
樹

The food's pretty amazing, too. Some of it looks like it belongs in a museum or something.

But the one thing I can never get over is how ***polite*** everybody is. They've got the whole thing down to an artform.

Please accept my humble apologies. I'd hoped to present you with a much more suitable "thank you" gift...
A gift?! You needn't have gone to so much trouble on my account! It is ***I*** who should apologize...

There are some things in Japan that I'm not so crazy about. For instance the subways: they get so crowded sometimes you can't even **breath**.

You've probably heard how expensive things are in Japan. Well, it's true, especially certain kinds of fruits and vegetables.

I stopped by the market and got a nice, ripe melon!
A **melon**?!! Darling, you know we can't afford such luxuries!

And to be honest, sometimes all that politeness can start to get on your nerves.

Thank you so much for letting me borrow your pencil. Oh dear! I've dulled the point of it quite a bit; Perhaps I should go sharpen it again for you.
Oh *brother*...

All in all, though, I think Japan is pretty cool. If you ever get the chance, you should definitely go there.

You have to watch yourself, though. If you stay there long enough you'll start to fall in ***love*** with the place. Even the weird stuff.

# TWENTY FOUR WAYS TO DRAW POOG

Celtic Poog

Siamese Poogs

Batpoog

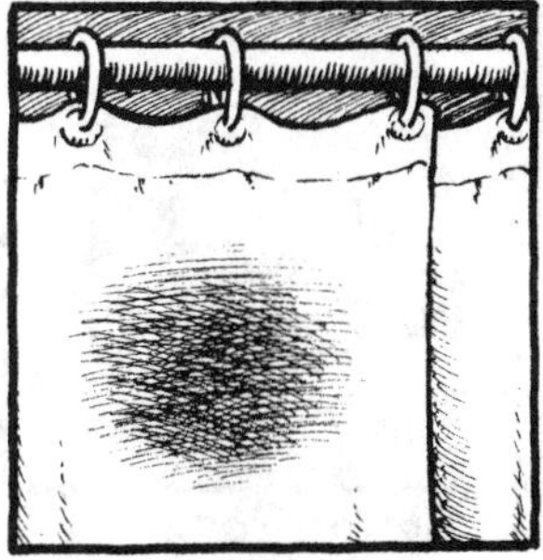

Shower Scene Poog

The Poog in the Hat

Cyber Poog

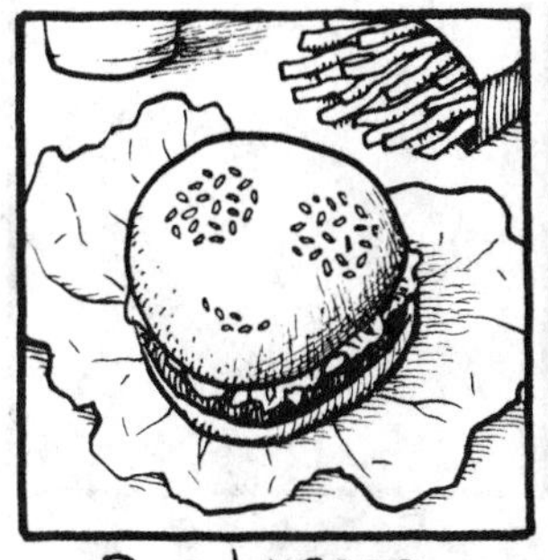

Poogburger

Poog Sushi

Poog Bubble

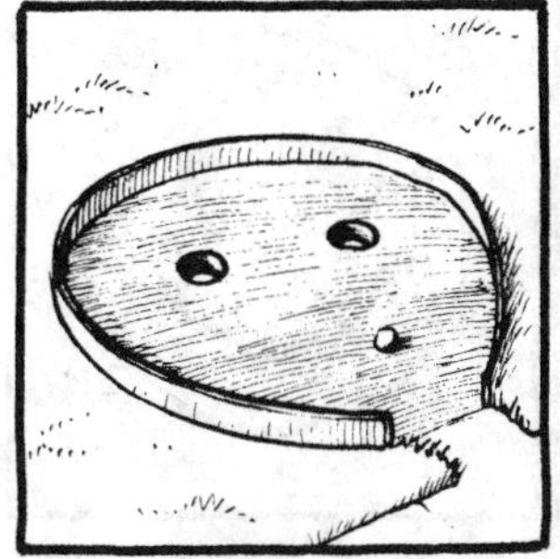

Putt-Putt Poog

Country Poog

Gorbachev Poog

Pirate Poog

Rat Creature Poog

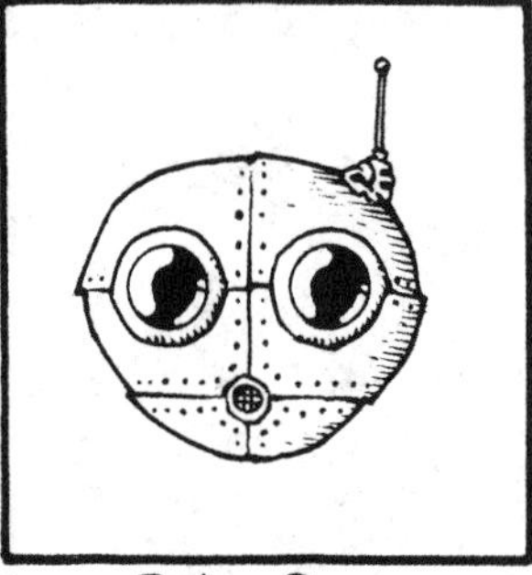

Robo-Poog

Tattoog

The Tao of Poog

Hello Poogy

Poogfish

Lava Poog

Poogsicle

Calligraphy Poog

Organic Poog

Have a Nice Poog